CONTENTS

Introduction

Welcome to the *No Limits Discipleship Journal*! You have embarked on a spiritual journey of great significance, and we commend you for undertaking this important step.

Let us introduce ourselves. Our names are Mickey Cox and Michael Ross, and we have been involved in youth ministry for a LONG time. We have a passion for helping students discover and live out what it means to be a disciple of Jesus Christ. It is because we earnestly desire to see teenagers grow to maturity in their faith that we wrote this book.

How to Use This Book

This book is designed for you to work through it with an adult mentor. It has been our experience that having an adult mentor is a critical part of the discipleship process. Prayerfully consider whom you could ask to serve as your discipleship partner.

THE BOOK IS DIVIDED INTO THE FOLLOWING THREE SECTIONS.

Section One—Discipleship Concepts

In this section, written by me, Mickey Cox, you'll find an overview of what discipleship is and how important it is for our lives. In addition, I've provided you with practical, hands-on instruction in various spiritual disciplines such as Bible study, prayer, living in community, and acting compassionately. Each of these disciplines will help you develop an intimate relationship with your heavenly Father.

Section Two—Journal Pages

We've provided you with several copies of journal pages that correspond to the spiritual disciplines discussed in Section One. While we didn't have enough space in this book to give you a year's supply of these pages, we're giving you permission to photocopy the journal pages, or you can download additional pages from <www.barefootministries.com>.

Section Three—45 Days of Devotions

I, Michael Ross, have written 45 days of personal devotions that follow the pattern of Bible study given in Section One. Each day of devotions have been written to help you put into practice the principles discussed in this book. Let me encourage you to start using the devotions as a part of your daily quiet time as soon as you receive the book. Doing so will help you better understand and implement the principles found in Section One.

Let's Get Started

We are excited that you have chosen to use this book to aid you in your quest to live a life of discipleship. It is our prayer that by the time you have finished this book, you will not only have learned and began to live out the principles of discipleship but also be committed to discipling others, teaching them what you have learned.

Are you ready to begin? We are. Let's go!

Discipleship Journal

No Limits

Mickey Cox and
Michael Ross

ISBN 083-415-0026

Printed in the United States of America

Editor: James K. Hampton
Design by: Kristina Phillips and Doug Bennett

ISBN 083-415-0026

9 780834 150027

Barefoot Ministries
Kansas City, Missouri

Discipleship Concepts

No Limits

Section 1

Chapter 1

Covenant:

The Ultimate Relationship

The Ultimate Relationship

If you listen closely, you'll hear it. It is the story of how God has acted throughout history, seeking to redeem the world. The truly awesome thing about this is that God chooses to tell it through those who have entered an eternal covenant with Him through Jesus Christ.

God has told His story through many people already. Abraham, Jacob, Joseph, David, Solomon, Ruth, Esther, Job, Daniel, Paul, Timothy—each of these folk played a special role in helping spread God's story to others. Now God desires to tell His story through you! God wants to establish His covenant with you so that His story will be told accurately, with wisdom and compassion.

Each of us knows that God loves us. However, I'm not sure that we all live in God's love. Let me explain. We allow so many things to get in our way of understanding the loving-kindness that God offers to us through His Son, Jesus Christ. The truly amazing thing is that no matter what we have done, His love is always there, waiting for us to accept it. In order to show us what this love looked like, Jesus came to earth in the form of a man. As He grew up and moved among the people, He demonstrated this type of love in every action and relationship. This love carried Jesus to the Cross where He was crucified—an act of love that for many of us defies explanation. Why would a good man die for those He had never even known? Because Jesus was also God, and He desperately desired to restore humanity to its proper relation to Him. This is the essence of true love—that God would give His own Son to die for our sins in order that we might be saved! No wonder the Bible says, "God is love" (1 John 4:8).

When we really understand and accept God's love for us, we can't help but pass along that love on to others. This is the Good News—the gospel! We need to share the love of God at school, at home, at church, at work—anywhere there are lost and hopeless people in the world.

To properly tell God's story, we first need to be involved in activities that will help us tell that story accurately. That is the purpose of this book. It is our hope to expose you to some practices that will help you better understand and live out the covenant that God has established with you. We also want you to be able to help others understand this covenant for themselves. However, in order to do this, we must first understand what this covenant with God means.

Covenants and *Hesed*

The concept of covenant is almost unknown in the Western world today. It is a concept that comes from ancient societies and still exists among some people today who are primarily in third world countries. As you read the Bible, especially the Old Testament, you have probably noticed that covenants were common. People established covenants with one another to serve as the basis for their relationships with others, whether it be individually, through the tribe, or even nation to nation.

The English word "covenant" comes from the Latin word *convenire*, which literally means "to come together." The Hebrew word most often translated "covenant" is *berith*, meaning "to bind." With these two definitions in mind, we can fairly say that a covenant is an awesome expression of committed love and trust. A covenant was usually made to define, confirm, establish, or make binding a relationship that had been in the making for quite a while. Once made, a covenant was for life.

Except in rare circumstances, the parties of the covenant always followed a set plan for how the covenant ceremony would take place. This included many steps, but the two primary ones were that an animal sacrifice had to be made and that there had to be a representative of each party present. These representatives would offer a pledge, a promise, to one another that they would keep the principles worked out in this covenant.

Once a covenant was established, it was to be continually worked out in everyday situations by both parties. *Hesed* is the Hebrew word used to describe the ongoing relationship of the parties in covenant, who worked out the principles of the covenant and agreed to keep its promises and responsibilities. Scripture translates *hesed* in a variety of ways, such as "mercy," "goodness," "steadfast love," "loyal love," and "kindness." However, the translation that is most often used is "loving-kindness." This really captures the essence of the covenant that God established with humanity through the death of His Son, Jesus Christ.

God, in His "loving-kindness," calls us to participate in this most intimate relationship with Him. This is not a short-term covenant. It is an unbreakable bond that we accept because of what God has done for us. God is the One who has done all of the work in establishing this covenant. Now He offers it to us to accept. It is in this new covenant with Jesus Christ that we are called to live out His story today. Jesus Christ stands as our representative in making this covenant.

Discipleship

Discipleship is the natural result of a person who has experienced God's *hesed* by entering into covenant with Him. When we accept Jesus as our personal Savior, we also agree to be obedient to what He would have us do. In Matthew 28:19-20, Jesus instructs His disciples with these words: "All authority in heaven and on earth has been given to me. Therefore go and make disciples of all nations, baptizing them in the name of the Father and of the Son and of the Holy Spirit, and teaching them to obey everything I have commanded you. And surely I am with you always, to the very end of the age."

Discipleship, then, is the process of learning how to follow Jesus. It typically happens one-on-one, as a new or growing Christian commits to meeting with another, more mature Christian (usually an adult) for personal accountability and spiritual growth. The goal is that the older disciple would be able to guide the younger disciple in his or her spiritual walk, helping the younger one discover the practices that assist in this walk, and enabling the newer disciple to grow toward spiritual maturity. In so doing, the older disciple fulfills his or her responsibility to teach others to obey every instruction God has given to us. And the younger disciple fulfills his or her responsibility to live out what it means to bear the name of Christ—that of being called a "Christian."

Over the course of this book we will address four primary avenues to help us grow as disciples of Jesus Christ. These are:

Contemplation—learning to read and study the Bible

Communication—learning to both talk to and listen to God

Community—learning the importance of being in fellowship with one another

Compassion—learning why we are called to reach out to others in need

As you work through this book, we invite you to keep a journal, a notebook of some sort where you can record how you are growing as a disciple. People have been using journals for centuries as a way to converse with God, study His Word, make commitments to Him, and keep track of how God has been at work in their lives. Using a journal is no magic potion for instant discipleship, but rather a tool to help us on our journey.

We have provided you with some sample journal pages in this book that correspond to the above four practices. These are located in section 2 of this book. However, due to the length of this book, there aren't enough pages for you to use every day. Therefore, we encourage you to either make photocopies of these pages, or download additional copies of the pages from www.barefootministries.com. You might even prefer to use a spiral-bound notebook and write in the headings yourself based on the pages we have provided. The key here is not how you create your journal, but rather that you have one. As we proceed through these chapters, we think you will begin to recognize just how important a journal can be in our discipleship process.

Your Covenant with God

Are you up for this adventure with God? Are you willing to make this kind of covenant with God to live out His story through your life as you learn to be His disciple? If so, let me invite you to read, carefully consider, and then sign the covenant located on page 11. By signing this covenant, you not only indicate your willingness to accept the *hesed*, the "loving-kindness" of God, but also commit to a process of lifelong discipleship. In signing this covenant, you are agreeing that you will live your life in such a way that God will be able to use you to continue to tell His story. The rest of this book is designed to help you do just that. In fact, it is in the daily living that the principles of the covenant, the *hesed*, are worked out.

While the commitment on our end may seem large, think for just a moment about the commitment that God has already made. Through His Son, God has given us the opportunity to live in relationship with Him. Through the Holy Spirit, God comforts us, encourages us, leads us, and makes us holy. No matter how much this commitment costs us, it cost God much more—the death of His Son.

For more information about the idea of covenant, check out the book *The Covenant* by James Garlow (Beacon Hill Press of Kansas City). It is a great explanation of this important spiritual principle.

Discipleship Covenant

Understanding that God has created a covenant with me and that I enter this covenant with Jesus Christ as my representative, I commit to meet with and know God more through an ongoing ministry of discipleship.

Because the process of discipleship is not a solitary activity, I also commit to meet on a regular basis with someone who has already been on this discipleship journey for some time and is further along than me. This person will help me bring to maturity the process of spiritual growth that God has already begun in me.

To help me come to spiritual maturity, I commit with my discipleship partner to practice the following:

- ❖CONTEMPLATION—the study of God's Word on a daily basis.
- ❖COMMUNICATION—take significant time to talk with and listen to my Heavenly Father.
- ❖COMMUNITY—engage in Christian fellowship with my brothers and sisters in Christ.
- ❖COMPASSION—explore ways to live out the love of Christ to others.

We, the undersigned, agree to the principles and commitments outlined in this covenant and understand that this is a lifelong commitment to one another.

Jesus Christ
Covenant Representative

Teen

Parent

Discipleship Partner

Date

Discipleship Covenant

Chapter 2

Covenant:

Knowing Where You Are Headed

Knowing Where You Are Headed

Whenever I start out on a journey, I always ask one extremely important question—namely, "Where am I going?" If I don't know where I want to go, I'll never know when, or even if, I've arrived. For instance, if I want to visit my friend, I need to know where my friend lives. If he lives in Phoenix, and I live in Kansas City, it doesn't do me any good if I travel to Toronto. I simply won't find my friend. Wandering around in circles might be fun in the beginning, but it will soon become a frustrating, doomed enterprise.

Of course, just knowing where I want to go is not enough. It also helps to take along someone who knows how to get to Phoenix. I can certainly read a map, and I might even be able to get there by myself. But the journey will be much easier, and much more enjoyable, if someone who knows where we are going is with me.

Just as importantly, I also need to take along the right equipment. If I visit my friend in Phoenix in the middle of the summer, I will make sure to pack summer-type clothes, plenty of sunscreen, a hat to keep the sun off my head, and lots of water. If I fail to plan properly, then not only will I end up with a major sunburn and dehydration, but also chances are I won't enjoy the trip and I might not even make it to my final destination.

Recently, I ran across a true story of a couple who didn't pay enough attention to their "journey." They were quite independent and over a period of time ended up where they really didn't intend to go. The following timeline is adapted from articles I read in the *Denver Rocky Mountain News* that weave a story that is hard to believe. Look at the map below so that you can follow along where this couple drove and see what they did wrong. As you read this story, I want you to see if you can identify with any of the things this couple did as you contemplate your own "journey."

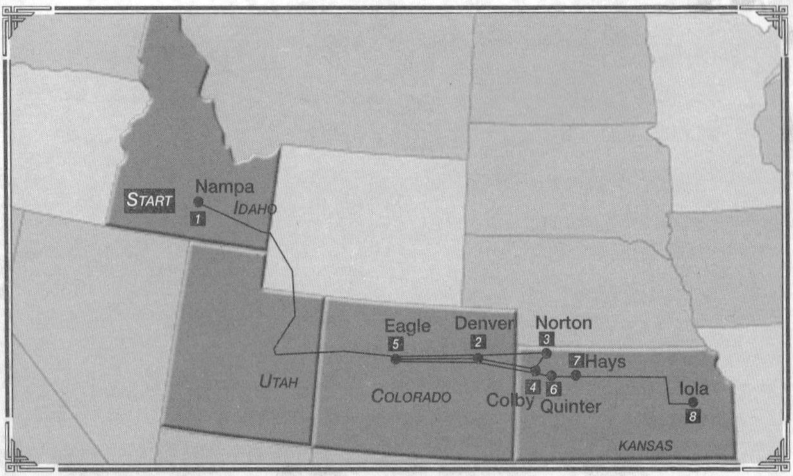

On SUNDAY, MARCH 15, Nellie and Orville Obendorf of Nampa, Idaho, set out for a surprise visit to Nellie's sister in Iola, Kansas, near the Missouri border of southeast Kansas. Nellie was 65 and Orville was 71. It happened to be his 71st birthday that day. They were retired farmers. They had no map or major food items in the car with them as they set out on this journey.

SUNDAY, MARCH 22

Having passed through Denver, Nellie and Orville drove northeast toward Kansas to skirt the first of two blizzards that had begun in western Kansas. After Nellie made a wrong turn in the blinding snow, their car became stuck in a ditch six miles west of Norton, Kansas. Once trapped, they used the last of their gas for the heater and huddled together for warmth under several quilts they had brought along, deciding to wait out the two blizzards that dumped over 36 inches of snow on their trapped 1981 Chevy Caprice with a white top. Nellie, being a diabetic, seemed to have enough insulin to survive the ordeal.

They began immediately rationing their eight cans of diet pop and a box of Girl Scout cookies. They ate a cookie each per day, but the diet pop lasted only for eight days. On the ninth day, because they could not lower the power windows of their car due to a dead generator, they took the radio out of the car dashboard and used it to break open the front windshield in order to get snow to melt for water. Nellie and Orville sat and waited as the raging forces of the blizzards by this time almost consumed them. They had to wait for 13 days before they could even begin to call for help, as they could not get out of their car because of such large drifts surrounding their car in the ditch.

SUNDAY, APRIL 5

A farmer was plowing out a road yesterday in the snow for the mailman when he barely noticed a white-topped car with roof-high snowdrifts stuck in a ditch on the side of the road. Seeing something move in the car, he stopped to see that two people were trapped in the car. Nellie and Orville were weak, confused, and disoriented after they were pulled from their car. They were listed in satisfactory condition at the Norton County Hospital.

TUESDAY, APRIL 7

After Orville's feet were treated for frostbite, Nellie checked out for her diabetes, and the front windshield of the car was replaced, the couple hoped to resume their trip to see Nellie's sister in Iola, Kansas. A Norton County hospital spokesman said that Orville would still need to be admitted to a hospital upon his arrival for further treatment.

FRIDAY, APRIL 10

Nellie and Orville Obendorf left Norton, Kansas, at 2:30 P.M. Wednesday, for what everyone believed was to be their continued trip for the town of Iola in southeast Kansas. The towns are about 300 miles apart. The couple ran out of gas, however, on I-70 near Colby, Kansas. A state trooper stopped and helped them later that afternoon. However, they have not been seen or heard from since, causing the Kansas Highway Patrol to issue an all-points bulletin for the Idaho couple. "I haven't heard a word from them, and I'm concerned," said Nellie's sister in Iola.

SATURDAY, APRIL 11

The Obendorfs surfaced, Thursday, in Eagle, Colorado, a community about 120 miles west of Denver and 300 miles from the Colorado/Kansas border. The couple spent Thursday night at a motel in Eagle, bought breakfast Friday morning, and headed out with Nellie at the wheel. Earlier, authorities searching for the couple had thought they were still on their way to Iola to visit relatives. However, it was found that after leaving Norton, they headed west toward Idaho instead. "They were very independent when they left here and wanted to do this all on their own," said an administrator of the hospital in Norton. However, now the couple is in the town of Quinter in northwest Kansas. Having arrived, they checked into a motel only to discover that Orville was unable to walk. He was immediately taken by ambulance to the Gove County Hospital. He is being treated there for problems arising from exposure when the couple was snowbound in their car.

SUNDAY, APRIL 12

A couple who drove back and forth across Kansas and Colorado for three days after spending almost two weeks marooned in their car by prairie blizzards were being guarded by relatives yesterday after they turned up only 60 miles from where they started. They had been missing since they left the hospital Wednesday, ostensibly to complete their trip to a relative's home in southeastern Kansas. They apparently decided to return to Idaho, but made wrong turn after wrong turn until they had driven about 660 miles out of their way.

"I just kind of felt like I was driving in circles all day yesterday," the 65-year-old woman said. Orville Obendorf was transferred yesterday again by ambulance to Hadley Regional Medical Center in Hays for further treatment and was in stable condition. It appears that after being treated in Norton for frostbite, the couple set out for Iola, but went the wrong way and ran out of gas near Colby, about 40 miles from the Kansas-Colorado line. A state trooper gave them some gas and pointed out the right direction. However, they never arrived in Iola, and authorities began a search. They were seen in Eagle, Colorado, west of Denver, on Friday morning and told a police officer there that they would be home in Nampa, Idaho, after one more stop. However, Nellie Obendorf, who has done all the driving through the entire odyssey, apparently became disoriented again and drove more than 300 miles back to Kansas, arriving in Quinter on Friday evening.

MONDAY, APRIL 13

Nellie and Orville Obendorf spent yesterday, Sunday, resting after their auto ordeal. Nellie was staying with her sister in Iola, while Orville was being treated at the Hays, Kansas, hospital for frostbite to his feet. "Nellie's just exhausted!" said her sister in Iola. Orville might have to stay in Hays from a few days to a few weeks.

TUESDAY, APRIL 14

Orville Obendorf was released from Hadley Regional Medical Center in Hays, Kansas, and was headed home to Idaho by plane yesterday. He was expected to check in to a hospital in Boise for continued observation. The couple's son was going to Iola, Kansas, to help his mother make arrangements for flying to Idaho.

FRIDAY, APRIL 24

An Idaho woman whose trip to Kansas to visit her sister in Iola became an odyssey of blizzards and wrong turns is hoping her airplane trip home today will bring an end to her troubles. "I just told my sister I hope they don't hijack the plane. That would be the last straw," Nellie Obendorf said. Her husband, Orville, flew to Idaho last week and was admitted to a hospital there for treatment of his frostbitten feet. They were amputated Wednesday. "He seemed to adjust to it real well," she said after talking with him. He is expected to remain hospitalized for several months.

His wife learned this week of another setback in their life. "We had a little bad luck. Somebody broke into our house in Nampa, Idaho, and cleaned us out, as if enough hadn't happened already," she said.

SUNDAY, JUNE 28

Nellie Obendorf, who along with her husband, Orville, made headlines back in April by surviving almost two weeks in a Kansas snowdrift, died yesterday, Saturday, June 27. Nellie had been hospitalized periodically and remained disoriented and weak from the couple's month-long odyssey.

I think you would agree with me that if this couple had done more than just have an idea about where they were headed, they could have arrived at their destination quickly and survived a lot longer in life than just a few more months. If they had taken a map along, using it to read the right instructions for traveling and to stay on the right roads without any disorientation, they might have made it. If they had kept in communication about their trip with someone who could have helped them when they got lost, they probably would have made it. And of course if they had listened to the community of people who wanted to help them complete their journey, they would have made it to the end a lot easier and with better results.

However, as I've reflected on this true-life story, it seems similar to the way many of us who set out on this lifetime adventure with God begin our journey. We start out with good intentions, but we don't have a clear destination in mind. We fail to listen to those who have traveled the road and know where we are headed, and we neglect to take along the right equipment to help us finish the journey. We think we know where we are headed, but with distractions, disorientation, and situations that we are not prepared for, we find ourselves struggling to stick with the adventure because we had not counted the cost and prepared for the journey.

Jesus said in Luke 14:25-33 that we who are His disciples need to place Him first in our lives—not our father or mother, husband or wife or children, brothers or sisters, or even our own life. Jesus calls us to follow Him as His disciples, totally and without reservation. We need to carefully consider what it will take to finish the journey—to complete the tasks Jesus has given us as His disciples. Of course, Jesus does not want us to blindly and naively commit ourselves to Him like the crowds who followed Him for His miracles, healings, and blessings. Instead, He wants us to count the cost of being His followers in the same way that a builder estimates his costs prior to building and a king evaluates his military strength before going to war. To be Jesus' disciples, we must be completely surrendered to Him, putting Him first in our life in everything we do.

So what do we need for this journey, this adventure with God? There are three essentials. First, we need to take along the map—God's Word. Second, we need to have direct communication with God through prayer. Third, we need the support of our community, God's people. These three ingredients give us all that we need for the adventure so we are able to face life and its twists and turns. We'll examine each of these in detail over the course of this book.

Are you ready to begin? Then, let's "saddle up our horses" and get on with the adventure!

Putting it into Action

In your journal, write out a personal letter of commitment to God. Let Him know that you have counted the cost of giving to Jesus everything, putting Him and His will first in everything you do. Commit to Him that you will use the right equipment (God's Word, prayer, and God's people) so that you can reach your final destination—being with Him in heaven.

Chapter 3
Contemplation:
Studying God's Word

The miner's cage, also called a "skip," descended quickly 1,000 feet down the Mollie Kathleen Gold Mine shaft to the "Ten Hundred" level in order for us to find out how $700 million in gold (by today's standards) had been mined. It was a 3' x 4' cage that carried seven of us down into the depths of the Rocky Mountains. Needless to say, we were riding "cozy" as we whizzed by different "drifts," or levels, to get to that "Ten Hundred" level.

In 1890 a prospector named Bob Womack, who was also a part-time cowboy, ended his long search for pay dirt by striking the El Paso Lode near what became Cripple Creek, Colorado. This 24 square miles on the southwestern slopes of Pikes Peak soon became known as the richest gold strike in U.S. history, and Cripple Creek was dubbed "The World's Greatest Gold Camp." Gold continues to be mined here even today. During those boom years of the late 1890s and early 1900s, Cripple Creek's population grew from 15 to 50,000; from 1 gold claim to 500; from no millionaires to 28. All this from just digging at the right place at the right time to hit something fantastic that changed thousands of people's lives.

As we finally reached the bottom of the mine shaft, we pried ourselves from the "skip." As we walked around the 10th-level "drift," our miner-tour guide explained to us exactly how all the gold had been taken out of the area's 500 claims. He went into detail about the working of pits and excavations from which minerals are extracted from the ore deposits.

Our guide's explanations of this hard-rock mine and the use of power drills for making shot holes for explosives grabbed our attention, especially when he showed us the dynamite and fuses that were in the mine. Since the 18th century, the prospector's experiences have been increasingly augmented by a firmer grasp of scientific principles and sophisticated technology. Ore deposits vary greatly in their physical characteristics and may be excavated by means of a series of horizontal, vertical, or inclined workings in ore veins. The various excavation methods, the ore's removal from underground, and the measures taken to support the mine to prevent cave-ins (of which one lady on our tour was considerably concerned about) are all activities included in the meaning of the mining term called "stoping" (pronounced "stow-ping").

In hard-rock mining, "stoping" includes drilling, blasting, and "mucking" to remove the gold ore. The miners drilled to make round holes in the solid rock so that the dynamite could be placed in the wall. Then they used dynamite to blast, loosening the ore in the hard rock. Finally, they removed the blasted ore materials (a process called "mucking") in order that the pure gold could be processed out of the rock. In Colorado, much of the gold is encased in substances called sylvanite, a dull gray, gold-silver-tellurium substance, or calaverite, a bronze-yellow telluride compound of gold and tellurium. If these other substances are not disposed of, you do not get the pure gold—the precious ore that everyone is after.

As our miner-tour guide explained these processes, my mind began drifting to how this process also applies to the way we, who are Jesus' disciples, get into, or don't get into, God's Word. Do you want to be a better disciple of Jesus Christ? Then dig into His Word. We often want the "gold" out of God's Word, but we are not willing to "blast, drill, and muck" to get to the "gold nuggets" of God's truth for our lives. It takes diligence not only on the part of the miner to get the pure gold out but also on our part as disciples to get out of God's Word what He wants us to know and apply to our lives.

I've found that we could take these three terms of mining and place them beside three terms we use in Bible study. They are:

- ❖ Drilling—Examine the Word
- ❖ Blasting—Explore the Word
- ❖ Mucking—Live the Word

Mining God's Word

In the same way that miners must drill into the hard rocks to find the gold hidden within, we must also mine God's Word to find the precious principles for living that are contained within it. And just as miners must blast the rock with dynamite to pull out the ore, so we must dig deep with the proper tools to get to the truth in the Word. Finally, just as miners take the gold ore out through mucking to get to the pure gold, similarly we must get rid of the worthless things and focus on the things of true value. Until we do this, we won't be able to hear and apply God's Word to our lives.

In the remainder of this chapter and in the next, we'll examine how this threefold process for the study of God's Word—the Map we need for our lives—can assist us in living out what it means to be disciples of Christ Jesus. In the same way that the gold of Cripple Creek changed the lives of thousands upon thousands of people, when we learn to properly mine the gold of God's Word we, and thousands more like us, will be radically changed.

As we begin this part of our journey, start by asking God to reveal to you some amazing truths that you have never discovered before when you've read His Word. Do you have a deep desire to be a better disciple? Then talk with God about it. Consider using a journal, a notebook where you record your thoughts, prayers, and concerns, as a part of this process. This will help you keep a clear record of what God is teaching you as you progress through this journey with Him. Our minds tend to forget over time. Writing down the things that are important helps us to remember them, and we can then reflect on what God has pointed out to us through the study of His Word. As we work through this process, it will be important for you to have your journal with you to write in.

The Process

Before we examine the steps of this process, take a moment and write out a prayer to God in your journal, asking for His guidance during your study of His Word.

Examine the Word

When we begin to study God's Word, we should start by reading the passage we want to study several times. This helps us get a good overview of the passage. For many people it is helpful to look at the passage using several different translations to see how others have interpreted the same passage from God's Word. For information on the various versions of the Bible, check out "Which Version Is Best?" article located at the end of this chapter.

Now break the passage up into major themes or ideas. As you read, ask yourself, "What is happening in this passage? What do I see? What are the facts? What is this passage about?" Look at what happened just before this passage and what comes after it. Ask yourself those "Who, What, When, Where, Why, and How" types of questions as you read the passage. What is the setting? How does the author feel about this passage? What was it like to be in his shoes?

Are there any words that you think are important? Who is the subject? Look at the verbs in the passage. Are they active verbs? Who is the person or persons doing the action? Who is the object of the verbs? Look for any questions and answers in the passage. What kind of literature is the passage—a letter, a narrative, a poem, etc.? How does the type of literature it is affect the way we interpret it? At this stage of your study, don't rely on outlines provided by study Bibles. Come up with your own main ideas.

In your journal, not only write out what you think the passage is saying to you, but also write down any questions you might have about the passage. Place yourself in the actual scene of the passage, and seek to live out the experience of the passage. Write out what you are smelling, hearing, seeing, feeling, tasting, and touching. And as you're writing out your Examine the Word section, make sure you're accurately noting only what is actually found in Scripture. Examine the Word moves us beyond just our rational, logical, cognitive, analytical approach to data. It opens us up at the affective, feeling level of our lives where we often need to hear the Word of God.

To help you better understand the principles we'll discuss, let's actually look at a passage together. Turn to Mark 1:40-45 in your Bible. Using your journal, dig into this passage, using the model described above, and pull out some observations that will bring this passage alive to you. Let your mind imagine being there with Jesus as His disciple during this experience.

Let's start by looking at the various translations. For instance, in the NIV it says in verse 41 that Jesus was "filled with compassion." Does this phrase mean the same thing as "felt sorry" (as found in the NCV and CEV versions), or "moved with pity" (as found in the RSV or TLB translations)? If not, how do they differ? In this example, does being compassionate mean the same thing as feeling sorry for someone, or does it contain a much deeper meaning?

Examine the major themes. The request of the leper, the compassion of Jesus, the need to share what has happened with others—these are all prevalent themes. Ask the questions discussed above. Who is the central character(s)? Here it is Jesus and the leper. What are they doing? The leper wants Jesus to heal him; Jesus responds by healing the leper. Why are they doing this? The leper wants to be made whole again; Jesus wants us to be made whole.

Jesus is the primary subject here. He is the one who does the healing. The leper is the one who receives the healing. As you study this passage, what questions come to your mind? For instance, "What is leprosy, and why were lepers so shunned by others?" would be a good question. Another possible question might be, "Why did Jesus tell the man not to tell anyone about what He had done?" What does this passage tell us about how we relate to Jesus?

Now place yourself in the scene as the leper. How would you feel as you approach this miracle worker you've heard so much about? Would you be excited about the prospect of healing, or fearful He would choose not to heal you? How would you react when Jesus touched you (a definite no-no during His day)? And when Jesus heals you, how will you respond?

Congratulations! You've successfully completed the Examine the Word section of doing good Bible study. As you can imagine, this takes lots of practice. But the more you do it, the more comfortable you'll become, and the easier it will be.

Explore the Word

The second part of the process is Explore the Word as His disciple. This section is closely related to the Examine the Word section. Here we begin by asking ourselves this question—"What does this passage mean to us as disciples?" Look back at the list of questions you created in the Examine the Word section. Can you answer any of them now? As you think about this passage, ask, "What does this passage say to us as Christians? How does this passage transform our lives as Christians?"

- As you study and think about the passage, consider asking these questions:
- Is there a command we need to obey?
- Is there a sin we need to confess or avoid?
- Is there a promise God has made to us?
- Have we learned anything new about God, Jesus, or the Holy Spirit?

Each of these questions helps us look for the key ideas the passage contains that are meant for Christians.

If we don't do the hard work of studying the passage (the Examine the Word section), then, because we are human, we are prone to not properly understand what God wants to say to us. Because of the sinful nature each of us is born with, we can tend to read the Bible with a slanted perspective, only finding in it the things we think are important, rather than what God thinks is important.

Don't just read one passage of Scripture without considering what the message of the whole Bible is about. If you do, it can lead to a lot of wrong interpretations. Each passage must be read in the light of the whole Scripture so that you can see the big picture and not just an isolated snapshot.

Be wary of fanciful ideas or impressions, especially mystical "revelations" that you think are from God, without support from the biblical text itself. When we read the Bible, we don't read it as if it were written just for us. Instead, our fellow Christians at church, as well as all the Christians who have come before us, help us in our interpretation of the passage. It is extremely important that we allow our interpretation to be checked against the interpretation(s) others have made. If we don't, we risk discovering "truth" that is for just us, something that Scripture clearly does not endorse.

To help you with this, after you've done the hard work required by the Examine the Word section and then have begun to interpret the passage in the Explore the Word section, check out your findings against what others have said. This could be done by sharing your ideas with others who know how to properly interpret the Bible, or you could look at a couple of commentaries (books to help you interpret the Bible) to see how your answers match up.

Now, taking the same passage we previously used (Mark 1:40-45), let's examine it and pull out the truths we see there. Ask yourself some of the questions from above. Use the Examine the Word points you wrote down to lead you closer to your interpretations in Explore the Word and what they mean for you as His disciple. Write your answers in your journal.

Well, you successfully completed steps 1 and 2 of studying the Bible. In the next chapter, we will examine the necessity of applying (living out) God's Word in our lives as His disciples.

Which Version Is Best?

There are so many versions of the Bible available that sometimes it is hard to know which one to choose. Each Bible version has something to offer the reader. All Bible versions fall into one of three categories. Let's examine them.

The first category is called the "formal equivalency" or "literal" translation method. This means that the version is literally translated word for word from the original documents, keeping as close to the original grammatical structure as possible. The *New American Standard Bible* (NASB) is the only version that comes close to this category. While extremely faithful to the text, this version may not always read well, especially for teenagers.

Other versions follow a "dynamic equivalency" translation method. These versions strive for accuracy with the original languages the Bible was written in but are also sensitive to contemporary language issues. For instance, the King James Version, written in 1611, contains language that would be considered outdated by the average person. Therefore, these versions, while remaining faithful to the original texts, translate thought-by-thought rather than word by word. They seek to contemporize the language and grammatical structure in order to make it more readable. Some of the Bible versions in this category include: the *New International Version* (NIV), the *Revised Standard Version* (RSV), the *New Revised Standard Version* (NRSV), and the *New Living Translation* (NLT).

Finally, some Bible versions are "paraphrases." These versions are not translations in a technical sense, rather expansions of the thoughts and ideas reflected in the original languages. Their primary goal is to restate the biblical author's thoughts in contemporary words and idioms in order to make them understandable to today's reader. You may frequently find colloquial expressions (informal speech forms such as slang) in these versions. They may tend to incorporate specific interpretations of Scripture or the translator's own theological views into the translation. Some of the Bible versions that fall into this category include: *The Message* (TM), and *The Living Bible* (TLB).

So, which version is the best? Rather than us attempting to tell you which version of the Bible is best, we think it is best if you discuss this with your parents, your pastor and/or youth paster, and other adults who can help you make an informed decision. It is our opinion that the particular translation you choose to use isn't nearly as important as the fact that you use the Bible on a daily basis.

Chapter 4

Contemplation:

Living God's Word

My heart began pumping harder as the coaster we were in slowly climbed to a height of 117 feet above the floor of the Worlds of Fun theme park located in Kansas City. I had been invited to ride their new roller coaster called the Orient Express at a special premiere before the park was actually open. At that time, the Orient Express bragged of being the tallest roller coaster in the United States, reaching top speeds in excess of 60 miles an hour.

The first hill is a 115-foot vertical drop at 55 degrees and goes from 15 to 60 miles an hour in 2 ½ seconds with a G-force of +3.5. For many people, their faces look very different at the bottom of the drop versus what they looked like at the top due to the G-force. Often, they look as if they have a Jim Carrey face job!

A special feature of the coaster, besides going upside down in loops several times, are the double interlocking loops, 50 feet high from the bottom to top, called the Kamikaze-Kurve. It is an indescribable coaster experience.

If you can't tell by now, I'm a big fan of roller coasters. I will go out of my way to ride one that I think is worthy to be included on my top 10 list. I love the ups and downs, the loops and corners, and the feeling I get from traveling fast in an open-air car bouncing all over the place. Because I enjoy roller coasters so much, I often travel around to ride different coasters. Who would have guessed that, as a teenager riding the Big Dipper at Joyland in Wichita, Kansas, I would grow to become so fanatical about roller coasters?

Lately, I've added two new coasters to my list of "must-rides." The first is the Viper at Six Flags Magic Mountain in Valencia, California. This coaster has a height of 188 feet and has a speed of over 70 miles an hour. This coaster is one of the ultimate rides I've found! It is also America's tallest and fastest looping steel roller coaster. You turn upside down seven times as the Viper's coaster travels through 3,830 feet of coiled steel track. It features three massive vertical loops, a corkscrew right at the beginning that makes your eyes go bonkers, as well as a head-over-heels double loop called a boomerang.

Then there is the Magnum XL-200 located at Cedar Point in Sandusky, Ohio. This coaster has a height of 205 feet and a speed of 72 miles an hour. This is the world's tallest and fastest coaster! As you come to the top of the first drop, where your mind and heart can't believe that you are really this high in an unenclosed coaster, you get an awesome view of Lake Erie. That view is short-lived, however, because you are soon hurtling over a long series of hills and through three tunnels before you come screaming to an abrupt stop at the end. This roller coaster is not one to be missed. Just recently, I've now heard rumor of a coaster in Nevada that goes 100 miles an hour! Anyone want to meet me there for a ride?

All of the coasters I've been on have some great heart-stopping surprises with dips and loops galore. However, when it comes to dips and loops and surprises, I prefer to only encounter them on a roller coaster. In my life I don't want to experience ups and downs the same way I do while riding roller coasters.

Dealing with Life's Ups and Downs

It was at a moment in my life when I was experiencing a lot of dips, loops, and surprises that I finally realized I didn't have to go through life as if I was riding a roller coaster. I learned that when I stabilize my spiritual life through the study of God's Word using our three-step approach (Examine the Word, Explore the Word, and especially Live the Word), then the rest of my life would fall into place. I could tell a difference in the way I responded to people, in the way I handled situations, and in the way I relied on God to carry me through difficult days.

The key was learning to use the Live the Word part of our Bible study process. When I was only studying Scripture in an effort to learn new information, I was missing the intent of the Scripture to transform my life and help me become a better disciple of Jesus Christ. As I learned to be obedient to the things God was asking me to do through His Word, I found that a new identity emerged from within me—one that differed radically from who I was previously. My new identity helped me to be much more concerned with living faithfully before God, seeking to serve Him in every area of my life.

Obviously, not every day is perfect. I still mess up. I still have problems. I still have to deal with those unexpected things that just turn your life upside down. But now, I have confidence that when I have to face those dips and loops that life throws my way, I don't face them alone. God walks beside me, helping me to face and deal with those problems. And you know something wonderful? I've discovered that when God is with me, those dips and loops don't seem nearly as death-defying as they did before I asked God to help me live out what it meant to be His disciple as He revealed it to me through His Word.

Living Out God's Word

Live the Word is the step in the process where we ask ourselves, "Now that I understand what this passage means, what will I do about it?" You see, whenever we study God's Word, we are always given a better understanding of what God is like and what He asks of us. However, having this information is not enough. We then have to decide what we will do with it. We really only have two choices. We can choose to ignore it because it doesn't fit our preconceived notion of what it means to be spiritual or because we aren't willing to make the choice God is asking us to make. Or we can accept God's Word, allowing it to change us inwardly, so that our outward actions are also transformed. Only when we respond in obedience to God's Word (applying it to our lives) can we honestly say that we are disciples of Christ.

It is important that we distinguish between the three steps of Examine the Word, Explore the Word, and Live the Word. Why? Because too many people jump straight to the "What is it saying to me?" stage (Live the Word) without carefully understanding the original context of the biblical message (which, as we found, happens through Examine the Word and Explore the Word steps). Of course, it is also possible that people can only practice the first two steps and never move on to the Live the Word step. When this happens, they become really smart about biblical issues (they gain the head knowledge) but fail to live out the implications of that knowledge (having the heart knowledge). In other words, they don't apply the Word to their lives. After all, what good is accumulated biblical knowledge if it has no effect on a person's life?

When we practice the Live the Word step, it helps us see how the Bible can relate to any part of our lives: school, home, family, work, church, friends, money, etc. After we have finished the first two steps, then we are ready to apply God's Word to our lives. We can ask the following questions to help us make the application to our lives:

- Is there a promise to claim?
- Is there a command to obey?
- Is there a sin to confess?
- Is there an example to follow?
- Is there a behavior to change?
- Is there an encouragement to receive?
- Is there an insight to gain?
- Is there an issue to pray about?
- Is there a reason to worship God more fully?

After you've gone through this process, write out a prayer or a covenant with God describing the specific ways you want to apply this passage to your life this week or at least within the next month. It's crucial that we don't procrastinate when God asks us to do something. If we do, it becomes easier and easier to ignore God's Word until we reach the point that even when we know what God wants, we just don't care. Therefore, don't put off what God asks of you.

Now, it's your turn to write out what God's Word is saying to you in Live the Word. Using your journal, reread your Examine the Word and Explore the Word notes on the Mark 1:40-45 passage that we previously used. Now write down what God is saying to you personally through this passage. What are the specific things that He wants to do in your life to enable you to live out what it means to be a disciple of Jesus Christ? Write those in your journal.

Now, let me illustrate how God asked me to apply this passage. As I examined this passage, two ideas emerge about which I feel God is speaking to me. The first is "How willing am I to involve myself with those who are looked down upon by society?" We have lepers in our towns today—not physically, but people who might be viewed as outcasts and seen as undesirable. This could include those with AIDS, unwed teenage mothers, homosexual couples, people who have a different skin color or perhaps come from a foreign country, those whose religious beliefs are different than mine. How willing am I to reach out and touch them in love, just as Jesus did?

The second idea I'm grappling with is, "How good am I at letting others know when God has done something miraculous in my life?" The Scripture says that this leper "began to talk freely, spreading the [good] news" (Mark 1:45). When God does the miraculous in my life, do I let my family, my friends, even complete strangers know what He has done?

Now these are the areas in which I sense God is asking me to change. Your areas of application, those areas you need to live out, may be different depending on where you are at on your journey of faith. The key here is not to come up with some great insight so you can impress others. Rather the key is to listen to what God wants you to do, and then to do it.

It's Not About Me; It's All About Him

So far in this chapter we have focused on learning to apply and live out God's Word in our lives. As we've discussed, it is crucial that we do this if we really want to be Christ's disciples.

Applying God's Word to our lives is important. However, just as important is the need to see what God's Word says about God. Not just about what God is saying to us, but what He is saying about himself. The Bible is, in fact, God's revelation of himself to humanity. It gives us a picture of God's character: His love for humanity, His anger toward sin, His compassion and humility toward the downtrodden and the less fortunate, His power to free us. Who we see God as has a direct bearing on who we see ourselves as. So when you read the Word and listen to what God wants you to apply, look for those insights as well.

It is critical that we move from just acquiring information as we read the Bible to being transformed by its message. We must allow it to help form us in every aspect of our lives, especially in our relationships to others. As you study His Word, ask God to reveal constantly His "pure gold" to you. How do we know He will do it? Because James 1:5 gives us this promise: "If any of you lacks wisdom, he should ask God, who gives generously to all without finding fault, and it will be given to him."

At the beginning of this book, you were asked to sign a covenant with God that indicated your willingness to be His disciples. Why don't you take a moment now and review that covenant? Go ahead . . . we'll be right here when you get back.

OK, now as we finish this chapter, take time to write out a prayer to God in your journal. Let God know that you are committing your life to Him to do with as He wants, even if it means allowing Him to burn away the impurities in your life so that the gold of God's Word can be expressed.

In order to assist you with the three-step process of Examine the Word, Explore the Word, and Live the Word, we've provided you with several sheets that you can use to help you in your study. You can photocopy these sheets or download additional sheets from www.barefootministries.com. Using the search engine, type in "No Limits" and hit enter. This will take you to the page where you can then download the replacement pages.

Chapter 5

Communication:

Talking with God

We live in an instant society. We want things to happen, and we want them now. Because of this, our society has created whole areas of service that are dedicated to improving the speed with which we can do things. Do you need to eat on the run? Try any of the multitude of fast-food restaurants available just down the street. Better yet, just pop a frozen meal into the microwave and presto, you've got a full-course meal. Can you imagine typing a 20-page term paper on an old manual typewriter? Of course not, because we now have computers that significantly reduce the amount of time required. Do you want to write a letter to your friend who lives in England? No longer do you need to send it by postal mail, knowing he or she will receive it in two weeks or so. Now you can just zip your friend an E-mail, and thanks to the wonders of technology, he or she will be reading it in minutes.

We want things fast and easy. In fact, sometimes we'll even settle for substitutes instead of the real thing if it means we can get it faster and easier. We don't want to deal with hassles. Just give it to us! It doesn't matter if it might be somewhat unreal; we want it now.

Let's look at just a few of the types of substitutes that have been created in the last 50 years in an effort to make life "easier and faster." Experimenting with mixtures of molasses, bran, and wheat, Charles William Post invented a substitute coffee, which he humbly named after himself—Postum.

Voilà! We now have a coffee-free coffee! It tastes like the real thing, but with none of the caffeine. And most importantly, it was instant.

Deciding that we needed something other than sugar in our coffee and food items, a company created Sweet'N Low in 1957. It dissolved in hot liquids much faster and was a good substitute for sugar. Right on the heels of this creation came a new cream-free cream called Cremora, which debuted in 1963. Think about it—coffee drinkers could have coffee-free coffee with sugar-free sugar and cream-free cream! Is this unreal or what?

In 1981 sweet-lovers were introduced to something that was actually sweeter than sugar—NutraSweet, which was another form of sugar-free sugar. It was a substitute that was better than the real thing without any of the negatives. NutraSweet tastes sweeter, but you don't get fat and lose your teeth by the age of 60. And if that wasn't enough, we've recently been introduced to Olestra, the fat-free fat. Where will it all end?

The truth is, we love substitutes, especially if they give us instant gratification. In fact, we oftentimes prefer the substitute to the real thing, especially if there is anything that might be disagreeable or risky with the real thing.

Spiritual Substitutes

Unfortunately, some of us think we can allow substitutes when it comes to our spiritual lives. Rather than spending the time necessary to build an intimate relationship with God, we try to get by on a few minutes here and a few minutes there. If we are lucky, we might even spend five minutes in prayer (of course, most of that time is spent asking God for stuff we want). Imagine trying to build a relationship with a new friend if the two of you only communicated five minutes a day, and the majority of that time you were asking your friend to help you with things. Chances are your relationship wouldn't progress very far. It certainly would not be considered an intimate friendship. Most likely, this "friendship" would have no real impact on either you or your friend.

The same is true spiritually. We must take the necessary time to allow God to form and mold us into His disciples (a process called spiritual formation). True discipleship cannot be rushed. It happens as God chooses to work through us, and as we are ready to receive and live out His truth claims upon our lives.

Listening to God's Voice

Prayer is a process of spiritual formation for which there is no substitute. It is impossible for God to shape us into the persons that He wants us to be if we choose not to converse with Him through prayer.

In chapters 3 and 4, we discussed how to listen for God's voice speaking to us through His Word. Now, in this chapter and the next, we will focus on prayer. It is during this time of fellowship with God that He often comes in unexpected and awesome ways to help us on our faith journey. Through prayer God often reveals to us those areas of our lives that need to change if we are going to follow Him.

As His disciples, God desires that we spend time in conversation with Him. Let's examine some of the biblical reasons why we should spend time in prayer:

- ❖ We should pray because Jesus set an example for us to pray (Mark 1:35; Luke 11:1).
- ❖ We must pray because Jesus taught us to pray (Matthew 6:9-15).
- ❖ We must pray because Jesus expected His disciples to pray (Matthew 6:5-7; Mark 14:38).

Communication

The A.C.T.S. of Prayer

Knowing that we need to pray is one thing. Knowing how to pray is another. Actually, prayer is one of the easiest things you can ever do. In fact, we're going to spend the rest of this chapter examining a model of prayer that anyone can use, whether you're just learning to pray or whether you're a prayer warrior. This model is based on an acronym using the letters A.C.T.S. Each letter represents a specific step in the prayer model.

The letter "A" stands for Adoration. Adoration is the purest kind of prayer because it is all focused on God, not you. Adoration is all about worshiping and praising God for who He is, not for the things He has done. It is a willingness to love God simply for being God. Even if God had never done or given us anything, He is still deserving of our praise. When we practice adoration, we are offering our love to God with no strings attached.

How do we practice adoration? Begin by telling God you love Him. Read Scripture passages such as Psalm 99:1-5 that speak about who God is. Reflect on the characteristics of God—His greatness, His majesty, His power, His love, His grace, and His sovereignty—and thank Him for these characteristics. You might want to focus specifically on one characteristic each day. As you pray, think about how that characteristic of God affects you, and praise Him for that aspect of His character.

Now you try it. Use your journal to write out your adoration to God, simply thanking Him for who He is. Go ahead, we'll wait.

The letter "C" in the model stands for Confession. When we praise God for His majesty and His holiness, we discover just how unlike God we are. We recognize the effects of sin in our lives and how that sin separates us from God. The prophet Isaiah had this same experience. When he saw the holiness of the Lord revealed in the Temple, Isaiah quickly realized just how unholy he was. "'Woe to me!' I cried. 'I am ruined! For I am a man of unclean lips, and I live among a people of unclean lips, and my eyes have seen the King, the LORD Almighty'" (Isaiah 6:5).

Of course, recognizing our sin is not enough. We who are disciples of God must also desire to have every sin cleansed and forgiven. In Isaiah's case, once he admitted his sin, then the angel of the Lord came and touched his lips with a coal from the altar, and in so doing, took away Isaiah's guilt and atoned for his sin.

Confessing our sins to God might seem frightening, since we know that the "wages of sin is death" (Romans 6:23). However, the apostle John gives us this incredible promise: "If we confess our sins, he is faithful and just and will forgive us our sins and purify us from all unrighteousness . . . My dear children, I write this to you so that you will not sin. But if anybody does sin, we have one who speaks to the Father in our defense—Jesus Christ, the Righteous One" (1 John 1:9; 2:1).

Confession comes from the heart. God is not being informed of anything. He already knows what we've done. However, when we confess our sins, we are agreeing together with God that we have fallen short of His will. Furthermore, we commit that we will turn away from our sin and turn toward God and what He wants us to do. This is the essence of living as a disciple of God.

Now you try it. Write out a confession to God for anything that might be standing in your way of fellowship with Him.

Thanksgiving is the word represented by the letter "T." Thanksgiving is the expression of our gratitude to God for what He has done. Earlier we stated that God was worthy of our praise just because He was God. However, we must also recognize all that God has done on our behalf and offer Him our thanks.

The Gospel of Luke records a story in which Jesus encountered 10 men who had leprosy. The men approached Jesus and begged Him to heal them. Jesus ordered them to go to the priests, and while they were on the way, they were each cleansed of their leprosy.

Think about this scenario for a moment. You've lived a significant portion of your life as an outcast because of this disease. You probably haven't been able to kiss your wife, hold your kids, or even chat with an old friend because no one wants to be around you. Now Jesus comes along and heals you. As you ponder this miraculous turn of events, what will you do?

In the case of the 10 lepers, while all 10 recognized what Jesus had done, only 1 of them came back to thank Jesus for this miracle! Can you imagine? Jesus gave them their lives back, and yet only 1 of them thought it was important to stop and thank Jesus for what He had done.

While it is somewhat easy for us to be critical of the other 9 lepers, the truth is that we often do the same thing. Think about all of the things that God has done for you. Now let me ask you a question—when was the last time you spent a significant portion of your prayer time thanking God for what He has done? It's humbling when we realize how many things God does that we simply take for granted. This is the reason for the thanksgiving part of this model—remembering what God has done on our behalf and then offering our gratitude to Him in response. In fact, the apostle Paul goes so far as to say we should "give thanks in *all* circumstances, for this is God's will for you in Christ Jesus" (1 Thessalonians 5:18, emphasis added).

When we offer thanks to God in prayer, we should think of specific situations, people, and things for which we want to give thanks. Possible items for which we can give thanks include our family, friends, food, and shelter; our pastors, youth pastors, churches, and youth groups; our unique gifts and talents; and our ministry opportunities. We can even thank God for the hard times in which we have seen Him at work both in our lives and in the lives of those around us.

Let's practice offering our thanks to God. Write out your prayer of thanksgiving to God for all that He has done for you and others.

Supplication ("S") is the final step in our model of prayer. This is the part of our prayer life where we make our requests known to God. It is in Supplication that we ask for God's intervention in both our lives and the lives of others. We ask God for these things because we believe He will do it. Three passages of Scripture help us understand why God answers prayer:

❖ Because He is our Father and wants what is best for us (Matthew 7:9-11).

❖ Because in the model of prayer Jesus gave His disciples, He instructed them to ask for those things that are essential to our physical and spiritual needs (Matthew 6:9-13).

❖ Because when we ask anything according to His will, it will be done (1 John 5:14-15).

We need to make our requests known to God who can and will help. In fact, the apostle Paul tells us, "Do not be anxious about anything, but in everything, by prayer and petition, with thanksgiving, present your requests to God. And the peace of God, which transcends all understanding, will guard your hearts and your minds in Christ Jesus" (Philippians 4:6-7). We are called to turn our needs over to God and let Him take care of them.

It is sometimes tempting to think that God doesn't care about our small requests. That simply is not true. God cares for ALL of our needs because He cares for us! Whether it be for the salvation of your friend or for help studying for your biology midterm, God is concerned and wants to help us.

As you practice supplication, try praying for others first and then for yourself. This moves the focus off what we want and instead places the focus on what God can do to help others. When we pray this way, a most amazing thing happens—the needs that once seemed so big in our eyes are now viewed in their proper context, and we begin to align our requests more with what God wants, rather than just what we want.

As you pray, talk with God about the needs of your church and youth group, school friends, and family members. Bring before Him the concerns that have been expressed by missionaries around the world. Ask God to intervene in the lives of the many people who still have not heard the Good News about Jesus Christ. And share with Him those areas in your life where there is resistance to His plans and purposes.

Now you try it. Write out your prayer of supplication to God, asking for His will to be done in each situation.

Many people have found that it is helpful for them to write out their prayers to God, like a letter to a friend, and place them in their journal. You might even want to keep a list of various topics to pray about in the prayer section of your journal, assigning each topic to a day of the week. As you use the A.C.T.S. prayer guideline, consider varying which step of the model receives focus. Spend one day entirely in Adoration, the next day in Confession, and so on. Be as creative with your prayer life as you are with your friends, because you're talking to your Best Friend.

As you finish this chapter on communicating with God and before you go on to the next chapter about God communicating with you, meditate on these words from the song "Shout to the Lord." What are you saying to God, and what is God saying to you as you sing this?

Shout to the Lord

My Jesus, my Savior
Lord there is none like You
All of my days
I want to praise
The wonders of Your mighty love

My comfort, my shelter
Tower of refuge and strength
Let every breath
All that I am
Never cease to worship You

Shout to the Lord
All the earth
Let us sing
Power and majesty
Praise to the King
Mountains bow down
And the seas will roar
At the sound
Of Your name

I sing for joy
At the works
Of Your hands
Forever I'll love You
Forever I'll stand
Nothing compares
To the promise
I have in You

Now It's Your Turn

We have provided you with some blank "Communication" sheets to assist you in your prayer time. As before, additional blank pages may be downloaded from <www.barefootministries.com>. Using the search engine, type in "No Limits" and hit Enter. This will take you to the page where you can then download the replacement pages.

As this chapter closes, we urge you to go back to chapter 1 and reexamine the covenant you signed there. Now, using either your existing prayer journal or one of the blank pages we've provided, write out a prayer to God expressing where you are right now in your relationship with Him. Be willing to admit where you've fallen short, and ask for His forgiveness. As you do this, be sure to thank Him for who He is and what He has done, especially regarding your salvation. Finally, based on where you are in relation to God, offer your request that you might grow even closer over the course of using this material.

Chapter 6

Communication:

God Talking to Me

It felt as if I was experiencing sensory overload as I sat looking at the front range of mountains! To say they were beautiful and majestic would have truly been an understatement. The leader at our spiritual formation retreat had just dismissed us to go and meditate on a scripture passage he had given us. We were instructed to pick out a spot that would visually say something to us about God and His majesty. Then we were to concentrate on the scripture passage to draw us closer to the One who had created us and was forming us into the person He wanted us to be.

In my hiking around our conference center prior to this experience, I had noticed a great little place that actually had a wooden log bench that faced these beautiful mountains of Colorado. On this day, the weather was great with a clear, blue sky above that seemed to frame the mountain range even more perfectly.

As I sat down on the bench, I felt surrounded by God. The smell of the pine trees, the colorful flowers that were all around me, the wild grass flowing over the hills—all these drew my attention more and more to my God who loved me and had created a way out of my sin condition through His Son Jesus Christ. Everything I looked at was speaking to me about Him—His love, His compassion, and His deep desire to communicate with me.

We were given instructions to not get distracted or allow our minds to wander, but to really give God our full attention during this special time in our schedule. We were also provided with a list of possible activities we could do during our meditative time. This list included: singing songs to God, writing out a psalm to God, creating poems to Him, writing out prayers to Him, as well as many other possibilities.

As I sat there, I began to sing some of the choruses we had sung in our worship service on our retreat. These songs really helped me focus on God's character. A couple of hymns came to mind as I continued to allow God to talk with me and help me relax in getting to know Him better during this time.

I next focused on some scripture passages about meditation. Joshua 1:8 tells us, "Do not let this Book of the Law depart from your mouth; meditate on it day and night, so that you may be careful to do everything written in it." Psalm 1:1-2 says, "Blessed is the man who does not walk in the counsel of the wicked or stand in the way of sinners or sit in the seat of mockers. But his delight is in the law of the LORD, and on his law he meditates day and night." And Psalm 119:148 tells us, "My eyes stay open through the watches of the night, that I may meditate on your promises."

The scripture passage that we were given to study during this time was Psalm 121. After singing some songs to the Lord that helped me focus on Him, I began digging into His Word to see what God wanted to say to me.

I had been going through a phase in my life where I really needed some direction for my future. Everything seemed quite uncertain at the time, and I was concerned, perhaps overly concerned, about what the next step was for me in youth ministry. As I read Psalm 121, I began searching deep in my heart and in my spirit for what God wanted.

The first thing I found was that He didn't want me to worry, but to place my trust in Him and not my surroundings. The scripture passage I was reading affirmed this: "I lift up my eyes to the hills—where does my help come from? My help comes from the LORD, the Maker of heaven and earth" (Psalm 121:1-2). I was not receiving guidance just by sitting and enjoying the beauty of the mountains and surrounding hillsides, although it was awesome and pointed me toward God. Instead, my guidance was to come from God himself, maker of all that I viewed. God's creation was to point me to Him and Him only.

I wrote out the thoughts God was giving me into my journal. Following that, I wrote a prayer to God thanking Him for telling me things about my future, and for helping me see that there were decisions I needed to make with His involvement. As I learned to rest and relax in Him, I began to better understand that during this particular period of my life when everything seem uncertain, God was still right there with me, watching over me and protecting me.

I closed my time talking out loud with God about various requests and concerns I had. God felt so close to me during this special time that I thought it would be good to just stay there on the mountainside and meditate all the time! However, I knew that if I did that, then God's work would not get done. This time of meditation was simply preparing me to move out from this mountain in order to be His hands and feet in a needy world.

I also intuitively knew that I needed meditative times like this on a consistent basis. I discovered that when I am able to temporarily get away from the hustle and bustle of life and focus solely on God, I am infused with His joy and direction.

Why Meditation?

In the hectic, noisy, crowded, and busy world in which we live, we need to take time to step aside and meditate on God—to put our entire focus on Him—so that He can communicate with us without all the noise around us distracting us.

Meditation is a practice that some may question because of the way it has been portrayed and used in today's society. However, as we've seen, Scripture makes it clear that we are to meditate on God and what He has for us. Jesus himself set the example for us. Even though He was one with God, He still spent time in prayer, not only talking to but listening to His Heavenly Father (Mark 1:35; 6:46). Meditation is simply a form of prayer that allows us to concentrate fully on God and what He wants us to do. It is fine-tuning our spiritual hearing so that we can recognize when God is speaking rather than us only hearing our own selfish desires and wishes.

As we saw in the last chapter, we need to communicate with God about the things that are happening in our lives. However, communication is a two-way street. We also need to spend time listening, allowing God to speak to us, so that we can better understand and live out His will for our lives.

Meditation can take place just about anywhere, even in our normal adventures of life. Taking the time is the hard part. We can choose anyplace to meditate on God, but it usually helps if we can find someplace where the distractions are minimal. We really don't want anything keeping us from our intended mission of listening to God.

When we meditate, we should focus all of our attention on God—who He is, what He has done, what He has said, and what He has commanded. That's why we start with His Word first. It is a written testimony of who God is, what He is about, and what He expects out of us, His obedient disciples. As we meditate on God's Word, we are reminded that He is right there with us no matter what happens around us. We begin to understand that our prayer life does not have to feel dead, but it can be a dynamic relationship with God that constantly draws us closer to Him. Simply put, the more we know about God, the better we will be able to communicate with Him. What will it take from you to get alone by yourself to pray and listen to what God has to say?

Through both example and instruction, Jesus taught His followers how to pray. It's time to take out your journal. Draw a line down the middle of the page so that you have two columns. Label the first column "Things to do," and label the second column "Things not to do." Now turn to Matthew 6:5-15, and list those things that Jesus says we should and should not do when we pray.

The 24-Hour Prayer

Too many people assume that if they spend five minutes in prayer at the beginning or end of the day, they have done their job. However, prayer is more than just a "thing" that we do. It is an ongoing part of our relationship with God. Therefore, we are called to "pray continually" (1 Thessalonians 5:17). And the writer of Hebrews encourages us to "continually offer to God a sacrifice of praise" (13:15). What does it mean to pray continually? Let's examine what your day might look like if this were to happen.

Let's envision a day in which we pray continually. We wake up in the morning and thank God for a brand-new day in which to know Him and serve Him. We take purposeful time to be alone with Him. We read and study a passage of Scripture. God speaks to us through His Word. We spend time in prayer talking with Him about our life, what we need, what our concerns are. We talk to Him about what He wants us to do and to be. We pray for others and seek God's work in their lives. And we close in prayer by thanking Him again for meeting with us.

Although our formal prayer time might end, our prayer life continues. We can continue to listen to God and pray all through the day's activities—as we get ready for school, we can thank Him for the clothes we have, the food we eat, and our family and friends. As we head to school, we can pray for God's involvement in our school, for any problems we might be experiencing, for our relationships, and for opportunities to reach out and show His compassion to others.

While we are praying, our attention might be drawn to the beauty of the mountains, ocean, hillside, trees, flowers, etc. We can take a moment to worship God for the beauty of His creation. When a problem arises at school, we can whisper a prayer to our Heavenly Father for guidance on how to handle the situation. When He guides us on how to resolve the problem, we thank Him. One of our friends mentions a family problem, and we take time to pray with them. We continue to communicate with God all through the day until it's time to go to bed. At that point we thank Him for the blessings of the day.

We can pray anytime and anywhere. Sometimes we can pray aloud, and sometimes we must pray silently. However, no one can prevent us from praying, even in a place where public prayer is not permitted, because God is always present with us.

Prayer Tools

A great way to help us when we pray is to compile a prayer list. This can be kept in our journal, on a note card, or even on our computer or Palm Pilot. When we organize our thoughts in prayer, it helps us better recognize the power of prayer that is available. A prayer list can help us cover all of the areas for which we need to pray. Keep your list where you will see it on a regular basis so that it will serve as a reminder to pray for these needs.

As we saw earlier, all we really need for prayer is the Lord's presence. However, there are certain tools we can use to enrich our prayer time. Consider using a worship songbook in prayer, for many songs come out of people's prayer times with God. Many people like to keep a journal of their prayers, writing their thoughts or lists out as if talking to the Lord on paper. Writing our prayers out or keeping a list not only can help us to better focus on the requests but also can serve as an encouragement when God answers. You may also want to use books on prayer, biographies of great people of prayer, maps of world mission areas of ministry that need prayer, pictures of those you are praying for, or other reminders for your prayer time with God. The key is to let these tools assist you in your prayer time, not to distract you from it.

Now It's Your Turn

God wants to communicate with us more than we will ever know. The question is, are we willing to slow down enough to listen, really listen to what He has to say? If we are, we will discover not only what He wants us to do but also who He is and who we are in relation to Him. That is the essence of discipleship.

Take a moment now to review again the covenant you signed at the beginning of this book. Now take your journal and just listen to what God says. Write down what He tells you, and commit to following what He would have you do.

Chapter 7

Community:

A Place of Support and Encouragement

A Place of Support and Encouragement

It was extremely dark at 4:30 A.M. as our youth group set out to conquer the hike up Pikes Peak. As I placed one foot continually in front of the other on the upward trail, I kept asking myself why I agreed again to do this annual hike with our youth group. After all, it was a 13-mile trek to reach the 14,110-foot-high peak! Then we had to go back down the same distance!!

On this particular occasion we had the largest group ever who had signed up to undertake this trip. I was surprised to see so many of our group wanting to submit their bodies to the arduous journey of getting to the top and back. The preparation had actually begun weeks before with announcements and what-to-bring lists. Those students who had hiked the trail for several years knew exactly what to carry and what not to carry. From their prior experiences they knew that there were some things that, while fun, would simply weigh them down and keep them from achieving their ultimate goal of reaching the summit. Since this was a day hike, we didn't take the full backpacks we normally took for camping trips. Instead, we carried small packs, only taking what we had to have, keeping them as light as possible so that we could traverse up and back easier.

Since there were so many new students wanting to hike this year, we had to pay careful attention to what each student brought. I was particularly humored by a particular student named Tom who wanted to bring a rather large portable stereo system on the hike. He thought he could carry this gigantic "boom box" on his shoulder for the entire 26-mile journey! (NOTE: This was before we had the convenience of portable CD players as we have today.)

Tom was not at all pleased when we told him he could not take his boom box up and down Pikes Peak. He repeatedly told us that he knew he could make it up and down and that it would be no problem for him to carry the box. However, we knew better, so Tom left his stereo in the van that was parked at the base of Barr Trail, which leads to the top of Pikes Peak.

The day started out beautiful! By the time we got to the top of the first major ridge, the sun was coming up and splashed rays of orange and red on all of us. I quickly forgot that I had said last year that I would never do this again, and instead hiked on, thanking God for the wonderful experience of being in His creation. Everyone seemed to be doing well. By now we had grouped, as usual, into three pretty distinct groups. There were those who had to make it to the top as quick as possible, those who were capable of getting to the top at their own pace, and those who really needed all the encouragement they could get to make it up and down. Tom was in this last group.

Our plan each year is that everyone makes it both up and down. However, we always had a couple of parents drive to the top on the back side of Pikes Peak, meet us on the top for lunch, and if needed, were more than willing to take anyone down who just couldn't make it the whole 26 miles.

As time progressed, it became apparent that we all were going to at least make it to the top! I was thrilled! We didn't have to send anyone back or tell anyone to wait at Barr Camp (which is about the halfway point on the trail) until the first group came back down from the top to help him or her make it back to the start of the trail. We finally all met on top of the mountain, had our prepacked lunch together, rested, caught our breath, rested some more, worked out some kinks in our legs, and prayed together, thanking God for the safety we had experienced so far.

Tom was the last one to reach the summit. An adult sponsor was watching over him as he stepped into the building on top of Pikes Peak for a rest.

It was apparent that since we all made it to the top OK, we were all going to make it down OK. We would not need any of the parental cars to take students down this year. And as our "fast" group became more and more impatient to get started down the mountain, we began dividing into our natural groupings with which we had journeyed coming up the trail. We allowed the first group to take off but asked everyone to stay in sight in the boulder fields until we all got down to the timberline. Tom was the last one to leave the top with a sponsor.

Since the sky had been a beautiful blue all morning, I began to feel a little funny when I saw some dark clouds off on the horizon. They seemed to be moving in a bit faster than I was comfortable with. I just prayed that God would keep us safe on this community hike. Needless to say, about halfway down the boulder fields, I began feeling raindrops and heard thunder in the distance. And where there is thunder, there is almost always lightning! I was concerned by the prospect of lightning on the mountain. Since there were no trees among the boulder fields, I was frightened by the fact that lightning typically strikes the tallest objects—which in this case was us!

As I looked out into the distance, I saw what looked like a dark curtain coming our way. Within a very few minutes, the weather went from a beautiful blue sky to a downpour of rain. The rain soon turned to sleet, then to hail, and finally to snow, and all couched in lightning. We later found out that this was the worst storm that had hit Pikes Peak all summer. Students were running for cover under anything they could find, which was primarily large boulders. Some students were not even close to any large boulders and were getting totally drenched in the wet weather. As I looked over the boulder fields, I saw students scattering everywhere looking for cover!

Then I heard the most amazing thing coming from across the face of the mountain. It was Tom yelling for me to come and rescue him. At first I couldn't figure out where he was, as the echo of his voice on the mountain was a bit indistinguishable. However, I finally found him and helped him to find cover under a major rock formation before the hail took over.

The storm lasted for what seemed to be an eternity. When there was a little break in the weather, we would run down a little farther on the trail to find more boulders for cover. Slowly we made our way to the timberline, inching our way down.

At the timberline we gathered in an open A-frame building and began discussing plans as to what our strategy would be for the rest of the day. We felt that if we could make it to Barr Camp, which was the halfway camp, we would at least be inside a dry, warm area with a fireplace where we could map out our next step. So, group by group we set off running down the trail to Barr Camp. Once we were inside, we were offered hot chocolate around a roaring fire. It was beginning to get dark out, which was a concern as we still had a long way to go to get to the bottom.

After much discussion from adults and students, along with guidance from the Barr Camp personnel, we decided to stay overnight in their lodge, even though we had not come prepared to do so. Barr Camp had enough sleeping bags for us to sleep in and enough food for us to eat to satisfy the rumbling stomachs we were beginning to hear.

As we all sat around the fireplace, drying off and warming up, I heard in the back of the room a sheepish voice that had been haunting me throughout the day. "I thank God that we all made it safely here and that we are a group again!" The voice belonged to Tom. Tom—who had come on this hike, even though he was unprepared. Tom—who needed some encouragement that day to make it up and down the mountain. Tom—who now understood the importance of working together as a group to survive in a storm on the mountainside.

The Importance of Community

Tom learned two primary lessons about the importance of community that day. Let's examine what those lessons were and why they are so important to us.

The first lesson Tom learned was that the group is often better able to make decisions than the individual. It would not have done our group any good if each person had decided he or she knew best how to handle the storm, and each one ran off alone. As a group, we were able to make the right decisions because each person was able to contribute some needed information to our conversation. The old saying really is true—two heads are better than one.

When it comes to our spiritual lives, the group also plays an important role. We need to rely on the wisdom of the community to help us with our major decisions of life. It is far too easy to allow our individual decisions to lead us in directions that aren't in our best interest spiritually. The community can help us by offering more information, often seasoned with experience, to help us in our decision-making process. Furthermore, we can look to others in our faith community as a model for our own spiritual walk. In an effort to grow closer to Christ, we can desire to emulate the devotion to prayer of one of the senior citizens, the Bible study skills of our Sunday School teacher, or even the absolute faith of a first grader. Having these examples all around us spurs us on to greater growth in our own lives.

It is in community where we also learn the most. The community helps us become better interpreters of Scripture, better communicators with God, and better servants to others because when we come together for Sunday School, worship, youth group meetings, or even our discipleship group, we benefit from the collective experience and wisdom of those assembled.

A second lesson Tom learned that day was that there is strength in numbers. Tom started this climb believing that he could make it on his own.

However, it didn't take him long to realize that he just wasn't as prepared as he thought. If it had not been for the support of other students and adult sponsors, Tom would never have made it up the mountain. Having someone who walked beside him the entire way ensured that he would also make it.

Again, the same truth applies spiritually. To be blunt, we will fail in our journey if we don't surround ourselves with other Christians. Having someone walk with us who has already been on the journey for a while is a great help. It gives us confidence that we can make it as well. The encouragement we need to keep going forward comes only from the community. Because the members of the community have "been there and done that" spiritually, they are better able to understand our needs and encourage us when we need it, challenge us when we need it, and generally be there to help us along. Reuben Welch, a former college chaplain, put it best when he said, "We really do need each other!" Tom never forgot that lesson about community that day.

Learning to live in community is vitally important. We can't go it alone. Instead, we must have a community of believers who are willing to help us with our journey. There are too many situations and experiences that Satan will use to tear us apart. The only way we can survive is through the blood of Jesus Christ and the encouragement of a Christian community.

The question is, to what faith community are you attached? Do you have a group of friends and adults you can go to at any time who are willing to lift you up, guide you, encourage you, and help you grow stronger through accountability? If not, you need to make that a priority.

Now It's Your Turn

Grab your journal and look up 1 John 4:7-21. As you study this passage of Scripture, using the Examine the Word, Explore the Word, Live the Word pattern we learned earlier, ask God to reveal to you the importance of the community of believers. After you have finished your study, ask yourself how you are doing in being a vital part of that community. What would God want you to do in this community? Close in prayer, asking God to give you insight into what you can contribute to your local community of faith.

Once again, we have provided you with some sample journal pages to help you in your times of community. These pages are primarily designed to be used in either a worship service or a small-group (Sunday School, discipleship, etc.) meeting. When you need more, feel free to photocopy these or download additional pages from <www.barefootministries.com>.

Chapter 8

Compassion:

Living a Life of Service

Ryan was looking for ways to connect. He had been involved in our discipleship ministry and through his contemplative Bible studies had discovered that Christians needed to reach out and touch other people's lives just as Jesus modeled for us to do. Because of this, Ryan was constantly looking for ideas of how he could be Jesus to his peers.

In one of his classes at his high school, Ryan began to reach out and develop a relationship with Daniel. Daniel was very active in the music department, as was Ryan. Daniel played drums in the marching band, jazz band, and concert band. Although Daniel excelled at playing the drums, he did have one handicap—Daniel was blind.

However, Daniel's blindness did not stop him from being the best in his field. He worked hard, practicing regularly to maintain that status. Furthermore, Daniel's blindness didn't stop Ryan from becoming his friend. They could often be seen eating lunch together, working on music together, studying together to maintain their high academic grades, and attending activities together outside of their high school.

As their relationship developed, Ryan began sharing with Daniel about Ryan's involvement in our youth group at our church and about Jesus Christ and what He had done in Ryan's life. Daniel was a bit hesitant to discuss this at first because of some negative feelings his family had toward the church.

However, as time passed, Ryan was able to develop a relationship with Daniel's mother and grandmother that opened up doors for better communication with them about the church and Jesus Christ.

In fact, Ryan was eventually able to bring Daniel to our midweek student Bible study. Once there, Ryan introduced Daniel to just about everyone so that he felt comfortable in this new setting. At the Bible study Daniel heard for the first time what Christ had done to bring us all back into a right relationship with God through Jesus' death and resurrection.

Several weeks later, Ryan asked me to meet with him and Daniel because Daniel was asking some questions that Ryan felt I needed to address. We met at McDonald's over Coke and fries. Not only did we have a great time together, but also I was able to answer the questions Daniel had been dealing with in his heart. Ryan and I shared about accepting Jesus' covenant—His death on the Cross for us—that would bring Daniel back into right relationship with God. Daniel felt he was ready to make this decision, and there in the middle of McDonald's, he asked Jesus for forgiveness and began a new walk with Him.

We now had a new dilemma—how would Daniel be able to study God's Word in order to grow in his faith? We gathered several different sets of cassette tapes of the books of the New Testament for him to listen to for his Bible study. That worked well for a while, but we soon discovered that to "turn to Mark 10:45" was not so easy with a cassette tape. Yet Daniel persisted in his adventure with Jesus and grew by leaps and bounds spiritually as he and Ryan studied the Word together.

That brought us to a new phase in Ryan and Daniel's relationship. Ryan came to me with an idea that really was exciting! Over the years, Daniel had collected braille books because of his blindness. Ryan felt it would be a great idea to provide Daniel with the New Testament so he could study the Scripture easier than he could with the cassette tapes. I gave Ryan some information about organizations that sold Bibles, including braille Bibles, and asked him to investigate the cost and see how we would go about getting one for Daniel. As Ryan and I discussed this project, we decided to keep it from Daniel until we knew what we could accomplish.

Ryan's report was a bit discouraging. Together we discovered that just one book of the New Testament cost several hundred dollars. I felt we needed to continue to look for ways to get Daniel what he needed for studying the Word. Ryan was invited to attend our monthly youth council meeting to present his idea to the group for discussion.

Although the cost seemed staggering, the youth council felt it was a project worth pursuing. The Book of Mark was the Gospel we chose to present to Daniel. The project cost was over $400. The youth council took the project to the total youth group for consideration and commitment, introducing it in the youth Sunday School classes where Daniel was not attending. It was received by all as an awesome challenge.

We gave the project two months, as we wanted to present the Book of Mark in braille to Daniel by Easter Sunday morning. Within that two-month period, under Ryan's constant watch care and persistence, we were able to bring in the needed amount plus some for a future braille book.

We all arrived bright and early on Easter Sunday morning. Several weeks earlier Ryan had invited Daniel and his family to our Easter morning musical presentation. At the appropriate time in the service, I called Ryan up to the front of the platform, and together we called Daniel up front. We explained the ministry relationship Ryan had with Daniel and talked about Daniel's adventurous walk with Jesus.

Then the time came for us to present our surprise to Daniel—his own copy of the Book of Mark in braille. Several of the youth group members brought the rather large books up to the platform. We also acknowledged Daniel's mother and grandmother. Daniel's face expressed shock and then great joy when he realized what we were giving him. He was so grateful that he was now able to study the Word on his own.

Ryan reached out in compassionate love to Daniel, and it changed Daniel's life forever. Through this experience, Ryan reminded me that every Christian needs to live a compassionate lifestyle. When we look to God's Word for direction, as well as stay sensitive to His leading us to those who need to know about Jesus Christ, lives are changed—just as the lives of Ryan and Daniel were forever changed.

A Biblical Look at Compassion

The Bible contains many references to reaching out and touching others' lives with God's compassion. In many of Paul's letters in the New Testament, he refers to specific people that he helped disciple and/or brought to know Jesus Christ. Paul mentions these people by name because he believed that to be interested in others is of utmost importance in our journey with God.

As we study Jesus' life, we see how He took time for specific ministry to others. In the Gospels Jesus is shown interacting with individuals much more often than He is found speaking to large groups. Jesus showed us that

He didn't come just to redeem the masses. He came for individuals. He was willing to come to their level and offer them something the world could not offer—true compassion. If there is one thing that sets Christians apart from the world, it is a heart full of compassion for others. When the love of Jesus Christ is alive within our spirit, we will respond to others in need. No longer will others appear "invisible" to us. No one can be a stranger who has a need.

One of my favorite Bible characters is Zacchaeus. I think I like him so much because he was short like me! His story is found in Luke 19:1-10. Zacchaeus wanted to see Jesus, but he was too short to see through the crowd of people that had gathered. Therefore, Zacchaeus climbed a tree in order to see Jesus. When He walked by, Jesus stopped, looked up, and spoke to Zacchaeus, inviting himself to Zacchaeus's home. This was a risky move because Zacchaeus was considered unacceptable by the "in" group of his day. But, because Jesus was compassion incarnate, His fellowship with Zacchaeus opened the door for Zacchaeus's faith to blossom.

Jesus made it very clear that His disciples' first priority is to reach out to others. John 15:17 says, "This is my command: Love each other." The responsibility to be compassionate isn't just a choice we make. It is a part of our identity as Christians. We simply cannot follow Jesus and not respond to the needs of others.

In Matthew 25:31-40 we are challenged to look at those around us with the eyes of God. We may have learned or even been taught to deal with people in ways that aren't always compassionate. Therefore, we must allow God to help us restructure our thinking and lean on Him for direction in this new journey. When we risk reaching out in compassion, love, and fellowship as Jesus did, we demonstrate our commitment to the Lord.

There are so many ways today in which we can get involved in our churches and youth groups to reach out to others: mission trips, feeding the homeless, forming health-care packages, providing tutoring, raising funds for disaster victims, etc. The key is that our actions must emerge from a compassionate spirit. What about you? Do you view others through eyes of compassion?

In your journal, write some possible ways you can begin looking at the people and situations around you through God's eyes of compassion. Be specific, listing names and the particular way you believe you can assist them with God's help. Be sure to set some deadlines for these ministry opportunities so that you actually do them.

In the Gospel of Mark, Jesus encounters some Pharisees who are accustomed to being blind to the needs of others. When Jesus heals somebody on the Sabbath, they are more concerned that Jesus has supposedly broken the Sabbath than they are that a man has been healed! Listen to the challenge Jesus gives them (and us) in Mark 3:4: "What kind of action suits the Sabbath best? Doing good or doing evil? Helping people or leaving them helpless?" (TM). Jesus challenges us to leave people helped, not helpless. What legacy are you leaving behind? Will people remember you as being a disciple with Jesus-style compassion?

Journal Pages

No Limits

Section 2

Contemplation Work Sheet

Contemplation

Date:

Scripture passage:

Examine

Explore

Live

Contemplation Work Sheet

Date:

Scripture passage:

Examine

Explore

Live

Contemplation Work Sheet

Date:

Scripture passage:

Examine

Explore

Live

Contemplation Work Sheet

Date:

Scripture passage:

Examine

Explore

Live

Communication Work Sheet

Adoration

Confession

Thanksgiving

Supplication

Prayer Journal for

Date	Request	Date Answered	Comments

Communication Work Sheet

Adoration

Confession

Thanksgiving

Supplication

Prayer Journal for

Date	Request	Date Answered	Comments

Community Work Sheet

Date:

Speaker/Leader:

Title/Topic:

Scripture passage:

Prayer for this experience:

Main points:

Application to my life:

Thoughts about my worship experience today: (What music, testimony, scripture has impacted me today?)

Things I need to specifically work on in my life from this experience:

Who do I need to go to today to encourage, ask forgiveness from, share scripture or pray with as my Christian brother/sister?

Community Work Sheet

Date:

Speaker/Leader:

Title/Topic:

Scripture passage:

Prayer for this experience:

Main points:

Application to my life:

Thoughts about my worship experience today: (What music, testimony, scripture has impacted me today?)

Things I need to specifically work on in my life from this experience:

Who do I need to go to today to encourage, ask forgiveness from, share scripture or pray with as my Christian brother/sister?

Community Work Sheet

Date:

Speaker/Leader:

Title/Topic:

Scripture passage:

Prayer for this experience:

Main points:

Application to my life:

Thoughts about my worship experience today: (What music, testimony, scripture has impacted me today?)

Things I need to specifically work on in my life from this experience:

Who do I need to go to today to encourage, ask forgiveness from, share scripture or pray with as my Christian brother/sister?

Community Work Sheet

Date:

Speaker/Leader:

Title/Topic:

Scripture passage:

Prayer for this experience:

Main points:

Application to my life:

Thoughts about my worship experience today: (What music, testimony, scripture has impacted me today?)

Things I need to specifically work on in my life from this experience:

Who do I need to go to today to encourage, ask forgiveness from, share scripture or pray with as my Christian brother/sister?

Compassion Work Sheet

Date:

Person and/or ministry Jesus is telling me to reach out to in compassion:

Things I can do to touch this person or ministry:

1.

2.

3.

4.

5.

Results of my reaching out in Jesus' name:

Compassion Work Sheet

Date:

Person and/or ministry Jesus is telling me to reach out to in compassion:

Things I can do to touch this person or ministry:

1.

2.

3.

4.

5.

Results of my reaching out in Jesus' name:

Compassion Work Sheet

Date:

Person and/or ministry Jesus is telling me to reach out to in compassion:

Things I can do to touch this person or ministry:

1.

2.

3.

4.

5.

Results of my reaching out in Jesus' name:

Compassion Work Sheet

Date:

Person and/or ministry Jesus is telling me to reach out to in compassion:

Things I can do to touch this person or ministry:

1.

2.

3.

4.

5.

Results of my reaching out in Jesus' name:

Daily Devotions:

45 Days with God

No Limits

Section 3

Day 1

Understand That God Is

"Who can prove God exists? I have a skeptical friend who refers to the Bible as 'a bunch of fairy tales.' She refuses to believe in God without scientific proof. What can I say?"

Examine the Word

You alone are the LORD. You made the heavens, even the highest heavens, and all their starry host, the earth and all that is on it, the seas and all that is in them. You give life to everything, and the multitudes of heaven worship you (Nehemiah 9:6).

Explore the Word

Read Exodus 3:1-15.

God's existence can't be proved (at least, not scientifically.) Believing in God and knowing Him personally is a heart thing, not a head thing. If a person's heart is hardened toward Him, then none of it will make sense.

To be honest, we can't prove the existence of some of God's more famous human creations—people like C. S. Lewis, George Washington, or King Tut. Photographs, dollar bills, and ancient artwork provide evidence that these humans existed—but not proof. Evidence points to fact. Proof asserts an irrefutable fact.

On the other hand, we can put a droplet of blood under a microscope and, through observation, give irrefutable proof (what scientists call empirical proof) of the identity of this fluid. We can even match it to a specific human or animal.

We can't give empirical proof that God, C. S. Lewis, George Washington, or King Tut ever existed. However, the weight of historical evidence not only makes it possible to believe in God's existence, but also makes it very hard to ignore. Let's look at some of the evidence:

—God is the sovereign Lord of Scripture who speaks to men through His Word, acts in His creation and in history, and involves himself in the lives of His people.

—God is the Shepherd who guides (Genesis 48:15), the Lord who provides (Genesis 22:8), the Voice who brings peace during life's storms (Judges 6:24), the Physician who heals the sick (Exodus 15:26), and the Banner that guides the soldier (Exodus 17:8-16).

—God is the Alpha and the Omega, "the beginning and the end" (Revelation 1:8).

—God is Immanuel, "God with us" (Isaiah 7:14).

—God is our Father (Isaiah 9:6).

—God is holy (1 Samuel 2:2).

—God is love (1 John 4:16).

—*God Is* (Exodus 3:14).

Live the Word

- **God can't be forced into a box!** While evidence of God's existence can be found in the records of all world civilizations, one fact remains: humans simply cannot grasp God by proofs. He is infinitely greater than what our minds can comprehend. We must approach Him with faith, trusting the will of the one and only God; the God who is "I Am."
- **God gives eternal life in Christ Jesus.** God demonstrated His love for us by sending His only Son into the world to die that we might live. In Christ, God himself suffered at the hands of men and for men, bearing the penalty for our sins and giving us eternal fellowship with Him.

My Prayer:

My Thoughts:

The Cosmic Connection

"How can God make a difference in my life? How can I know for sure that He really cares about me?"

Examine the Word

I will make you into a great nation and I will bless you; I will make your name great, and you will be a blessing (Genesis 12:2).

Explore the Word

Read Genesis 12:1-9.

The journey ahead seems scary, yet Abram is obedient.

The Lord tells him, "Leave your country, your people and your father's household and go to the land I will show you" (12:1). The 75-year-old man and his family pull up their roots, step out of their comfort zone, and set off on a radical journey.

"I will make you into a great nation and I will bless you," the Lord promises Abram. "I will make your name great, and you will be a blessing" (12:2).

Abram embraces the unknown. He and his family travel through a hostile land, where there is famine and death. But Abram is patient and holds firm to his faith.

God prospers Abram—and fulfills His promise.

A promise from heaven whispered into the heart of a human—and the divine journey begins. That's the way a life with God starts. A Voice says, "Follow Me." If the human is obedient to God's will, he or she gets up and follows.

God chose Abram—one lonely man to be the foundation of a new humanity. God spoke, and Abram did what God said. He stepped into the unknown with nothing to guide him but a Voice—and the hope he put in his Creator.

The words have been spoken to you. Are you listening? How will you answer? If you follow, you will find what Abram discovered: What he left behind was nothing compared to what lay ahead. You will walk on a path filled with the solid promises of God.

God promised Abram that the entire world would be blessed because of what he did. Your promise is that your life will take on greater meaning—a whole new purpose for living. You will have a whole new power to live in the joy of sins forgiven and wounds healed. You will have a whole new degree of strength for the moment and hope for tomorrow.

Live the Word

- **When the Lord opens doors—be faithful.** That's what being a Christian is all about. You don't have to be perfect to make an impact—just obedient.
- **Listen patiently.** These times may draw out and stretch our faith. He has promised to speak to our hearts, so we can expect Him to, but He is not compelled to tell us everything we want to know the moment we desire the information.

My Prayer:

My Thoughts:

Day 3

Jesus, the Savior

"I encounter so many skeptics who refuse to believe that Jesus is Lord and Savior. How can I know for sure that Christ is who He claims to be?"

Examine the Word

Therefore, my brothers, I want you to know that through Jesus the forgiveness of sins is proclaimed to you. Through him everyone who believes is justified from everything you could not be justified from by the law of Moses (Acts 13:38-39).

Explore the Word

Read Luke 5:17-26.

"Who is this man?"

"The real question is, who does *he* think he is?"

The teachers of the law had heard that Jesus was in town, stirring up the crowds with His radical ideas. A few of the skeptical religious leaders (known as the Pharisees) had to hear it for themselves—so they made their way into a crowded building and listened with disgust.

The young Jew before them claims to be the Messiah. He even insists that He has all authority on earth, yet He wanders the land like a drifter. What's more, He's a mere carpenter's son and hangs out with society's undesirables: lepers, beggars, prostitutes, traitors, children.

Suddenly . . . CREAK! SNAP! CRASH! Wood breaks, clay falls, dust rises. The Pharisees glare. Jesus smiles.

A paralytic is lowered from the roof and gently placed at Christ's feet.

"Son," Jesus says, "your sins are forgiven."

"Why does this fellow talk like that?" wonders a teacher of the law. *"He's blaspheming! Who can forgive sins but God alone?"*

Jesus looks at the Pharisee. "Why are you thinking these things?" He asks. "But that you may know that the Son of Man has authority on earth to forgive sins . . ."

Jesus turns to the crippled man. "I tell you, get up, take your mat and go home."

A miracle! The crowd gasps as the paralytic stands up and walks out the door. Everyone in the room rejoices. The teachers of the law are stunned.

"Is this man truly who he claims to be?"

Jesus came to heal our crippled, sinful lives:

- ❖ "God made him who had no sin to be sin for us, so that in him we might become the righteousness of God" (2 Corinthians 5:21).
- ❖ "He committed no sin, and no deceit was found in his mouth" (1 Peter 2:22).
- ❖ "But you know that he appeared so that he might take away our sins. And in him is no sin" (1 John 3:5).

Christ had to be without sin to qualify as the perfect sacrifice for the sin of mankind—the perfect sacrifice for your sin. As God's sinless Sacrifice, Jesus made it possible for you to trust Him and be forgiven. Does He have your attention? Do you trust Him? Do you want to be like Him?

Live the Word

- ❖ **Make sure that your heart is sincere—that you truly believe that Christ is who He says He is.** Do a little soul-searching . . . and ask God to help you work through any doubts that you may have.
- ❖ **Follow the instruction of Hebrews 12:2:** "Let us fix our eyes on Jesus, the author and perfecter of our faith, who for the joy set before him endured the cross, scorning its shame, and sat down at the right hand of the throne of God."

MY PRAYER:

MY THOUGHTS:

The Sacraments

"When we take Holy Communion, do we really 'eat Christ's flesh' and 'drink His blood'?

Examine the Word

For I received from the Lord what I also passed on to you: The Lord Jesus, on the night he was betrayed, took bread, and when he had given thanks, he broke it and said, "This is my body, which is for you; do this in remembrance of me." In the same way, after supper he took the cup, saying, "This cup is the new covenant in my blood; do this, whenever you drink it, in remembrance of me." For whenever you eat this bread and drink this cup, you proclaim the Lord's death until he comes (1 Corinthians 11:23-26).

Explore the Word

Read John 6:41-59.

"Eat my flesh; drink my blood."

This is one of the most important instructions for Christians in the entire Bible. Unfortunately, many people have completely misunderstood it. In fact, some have even accused Christians of being cannibals! What they don't quite grasp is that this is the number one ingredient in the life of any believer in Jesus Christ.

Our spiritual food is Jesus Christ. In other words, we have to spiritually eat Him. We have to digest Him and allow Him to become incorporated into our spiritual being. He wants to draw so close and love us so deeply that He starts to become a part of us. It is this oneness with Him that gives us overwhelming love, peace, and joy. It is this intimacy with Him that gives us abundant life. But if we refuse to commune and have fellowship with Jesus, we end up starving spiritually. And with starvation comes spiritual death.[1]

Live the Word

❖ **Stop dining with the devil.** Satan will use every lie he can dream up to convince you that there is no power through Jesus Christ. He wants you to believe that nothing has changed inside you, that you can't have victory over sin. Stop the devil in his tracks. Draw closer to Jesus.

❖ **Don't be satisfied with "McFaith"**—making TV, movies, music, and gabbing on the phone your priorities. Choose solid spiritual food: praying, Bible reading, attending church—seeking an intimate, growing relationship with Jesus. Consider this level of commitment the next time you take Holy Communion. Make your prayer, "Lord, consume my life."

My Prayer:

My Thoughts:

Day 5

Intimacy with the Almighty

"God seems so distant to me. How can I learn to trust Him?"

Examine the Word

Create in me a pure heart, O God, and renew a steadfast spirit within me. Do not cast me from your presence or take your Holy Spirit from me. Restore to me the joy of your salvation and grant me a willing spirit, to sustain me (Psalm 51:10-12).

Explore the Word

Read Psalm 51.

God is God. His thoughts are not our thoughts. His ways are not our ways. Yet He loves us so much, He pardons our sinful souls and gives us a fresh start. He hits the delete key on the computer—and the screen is blank.

As King David discovered, God actually tears down that "giant invisible wall" that separates us from Him.

Are you carrying a huge load of guilt and shame in your life? The Almighty wants to remove the sin barrier. He is reaching out to you with open arms—go to Him in prayer. Tell Him all about your sins, tell Him you're sorry, repent of them, and He'll forgive you. In the Lord, you'll find acceptance, love, and freedom—despite your shortcomings.

Live the Word

- **Don't drown in sin.** Understand three truths. (1) You can't swim against the tide of God and survive. But you can come to the surface and cry out, "Abba, Father," and He'll set you on the right course. (2) Not one person on this planet is outside the reach of God's love. (3) Even if you can't begin to fathom the depth of your sin—Jesus understands. And He forgives you.

- **Restore your relationship; admit your sins.** Take a long, honest look at sin in your life, then tell Jesus Christ that you're sorry (make sure you mean it). Once you've confessed the sin and asked Him to help you change (called repentance), you can stop flogging yourself. You're totally forgiven. Now with your relationship fully restored with God, you can take steps toward growth and change. (The Holy Spirit will help you.)
- **Know who to trust.** Best-selling author Max Lucado has a simple strategy for trusting God. In his book *He Still Moves Stones*, Max writes: "Take Jesus at His word. Learn that when He says something, it happens. When He says we're forgiven, let's unload the guilt. When He says we're valuable, let's believe Him. When He says we're provided for, let's stop worrying."[2]
- **Know that following Christ is not a passing fad.** It's a step-by-step, day-by-day *commitment*. And like any relationship, it requires your time and devotion in order for it to grow. "Test everything. Hold on to the good. Avoid every kind of evil" (1 Thessalonians 5:21-22).

MY PRAYER:

MY THOUGHTS:

Day 6

Honesty

"I can't stand hypocrites—yet I'm guilty of being one. Sometimes I put people down, I cheat, and I even lie. I don't want to blow my witness. How can I get my life on track?"

Examine the Word

Then Peter said, "Ananias, how is it that Satan has so filled your heart that you have lied to the Holy Spirit and have kept for yourself some of the money you received for the land? Didn't it belong to you before it was sold? And after it was sold, wasn't the money at your disposal? What made you think of doing such a thing? You have not lied to men but to God" (Acts 5:3-4).

Explore the Word

Read Acts 5:1-11.

There probably isn't a person alive who hasn't thought he or she could get away with something because no one would see. Guess what? God sees every action and hears every word. Though He's quick to offer forgiveness when we ask for it, one thing is sure: We can't hide from God—not now, not ever.

Is honesty important to you? Deep down inside, do you want to do what's right and please God? If you just nodded yes—GREAT! But keep in mind that nearly every day you're faced with choices that show the world—and God—your honest answer. The temptation to steal, to stretch the truth (or tell only half of it), and to cheat is always staring you in the face. Unless you consciously decide to make integrity a priority, sin will push you over the line.

It's as if there's a tug-of-war going on inside you. Unless you have given yourself entirely over to God and allow Him to cleanse your sinful nature, there will be a continuous battle between what you want and what God wants.

So, how do you maintain honesty and integrity in your life? Answer: It all starts with prayer.

Live the Word

- **Ask God for help.** Pray something like this: "Lord, please forgive me for the sins I've committed. Clean up my life. Help me to choose honesty and integrity. I'm taking Your hand right now . . . and I'm trusting You. Amen."
- **Know the truth:** A pure mind is not a mind free of temptation. A pure mind chooses to act in the right way when temptation strikes. Or to put it another way, temptation is inevitable; what counts is how you meet it. Keep in mind that a person can be good without being faithful, and faithful without being good. What will it take for you to combine both?

  a. A stronger desire to be good

  b. A greater sense that faithfulness will be rewarded

  c. Friends who have the same goal

  d. A swift kick in the pants

  e. Confessing past wrongs to God so I can start over

  f. Another person or two to help me stay on track on a weekly basis

  Answer: While each is important, *e* is the first, and most important, step.
- **Examine Matthew 25:14-30.** Try to imagine one day seeing Jesus Christ face-to-face. Do you want to hear Him say to you the words the man said to his servants?

My Prayer:

My Thoughts:

Day 7

Purity

"I've blown it in the past—yet God calls me to be pure. If I choose to live right from this day forward, will the Lord consider me to be pure?"

Examine the Word

Dear friends, now we are children of God, and what we will be has not yet been made known. But we know that when he appears, we shall be like him, for we shall see him as he is. Everyone who has this hope in him purifies himself, just as he is pure (1 John 3:2-3).

Explore the Word

Read 2 Samuel 13:1-22.

Today's passage makes you a bit queasy, doesn't it? Actually, very queasy! What caused Amnon to be so twisted? Let's go back and reread 2 Samuel 13:3: "Now Amnon had a friend named Jonadab son of Shimeah, David's brother. Jonadab was a very shrewd man."

In other words, Jonadab was the long-toothed vampire in Amnon's worst nightmare. His sick-minded advice destroyed Amnon's moral purity and deeply hurt Amnon's family. To top it off, Jonadab's friendship cost Amnon his life.

God wants you wide-eyed and sober on this issue. First John 3:3 says: "Everyone who has this hope in him purifies himself, just as he is pure." Translation: If you claim to be a Christian, then purity must be your lifestyle.

Understand this: Sin is disobedience to God's will and the implementation of our own plan. When we rebel against God, it's as if our actions say that He doesn't know what He's talking about, His Word is outdated, and He isn't trustworthy. But when we choose a life of purity and trust His will—even in small ways—we bring Him glory. Our actions say that His commands are good and that He deserves to be obeyed.

Bottom line: If we want God's blessing on our lives, if we want to know Him intimately and be an effective witness for Him, submission to His will and His Word is nonnegotiable. (Check out Deuteronomy 4:2.)

Live the Word

- **Resist—and win the sin tug-of-war!** Know that God can use our trials to make us more like Jesus. (Check out James 1:2-4 for more on this topic.)
- **Make a pact for purity with God.** Ask Him for the strength to honor Him and to remain pure.
- **Saturate your brain with the stuff of God, such as Scripture.** Ephesians 5:1-7, Ephesians 6:10-18, and Philippians 3:12-14 are some good verses to think on—even to memorize!
- **Don't play with temptation.** It's a sure way to lose your balance—and, ultimately, the tug-of-war. Tell yourself this, "If I resist the temptation to compromise my values, then I don't have to worry about getting into trouble. With Christ's help, I'm living by a higher standard."

My Prayer:

My Thoughts:

Holiness

"How can an imperfect, sin-saturated person like me pursue a life of holiness?"

Examine the Word

"Holy, holy, holy is the LORD Almighty; the whole earth is full of his glory" (Isaiah 6:3).

Explore the Word

Read Isaiah 6:1-8.

While praying in the Temple, Isaiah has a vision of God. When Isaiah understands God's holiness, he recognizes that by comparison he is just a sin-saturated person. His sin is the opposite of God's holiness. The two cannot coexist. This is the reason for his cry of fear—"Woe is me!" (RSV).

Isaiah can do nothing to compensate for his sinful life. But God can. One of God's angels comes over and touches Isaiah's lips with a live coal, signifying that Isaiah has been cleansed from his sins and his guilt. Now he is pure in his heart and willing to answer God's call upon his life.

When you first encountered the living God, every sin in your life was revealed. But God, through Jesus Christ, forgave you of your sins and enabled you to start a new life rooted in His love and grace. Through Christ, you are holy—set apart from the world and called to be different. Your values are not the same as the world in which you live. You're becoming more like Jesus and less like the world. But, like Isaiah, we can't do it on our own.

Listen to God's promise: "You are to be holy to me because I, the LORD, am holy, and I have set you apart from the nations to be my own" (Leviticus 20:26). Did you catch it? Because God is holy, we who are in relationship to God can also live holy lives through Him! It is God who makes us holy! But what does this mean?

If you are holy, you . . .

... choose righteousness even when you can get away with sin.

... forget what's behind and press toward the goal of serving Jesus here on earth and seeing Him in heaven.

... trust Jesus—even when life doesn't make sense. (Check out Hebrews 11:36-40.)

... seek to live in such a way that you reflect God in all that you do and say.

Does this describe your life? If not, God is waiting to make you holy. How does God make you holy? When you confess your need to God and surrender yourself to His will, God fills you with His Holy Spirit. God cleanses the sinful nature (original sin) from your heart. God, through the Holy Spirit, then gives you power to live for and serve Him. This is holiness—you surrender yourself completely to God, and He sanctifies you, sets you apart, for His purpose.

Live the Word

- **Strive to consistently walk your talk.** Be a promise keeper—the trustworthy guy or girl who others can count on. Holiness is both an inward and outward characteristic. Others should be able to see Jesus in your actions and speech.
- **Follow the Bible's instructions on how to live:** "Be imitators of God, therefore, as dearly loved children and live a life of love, just as Christ loved us and gave himself up for us as a fragrant offering and sacrifice to God" (Ephesians 5:1-2).

MY PRAYER:

MY THOUGHTS:

Knowing and Doing God's Will

"How can I get a clue about God's will?"

Examine the Word

Therefore, I urge you, brothers, in view of God's mercy, to offer your bodies as living sacrifices, holy and pleasing to God—this is your spiritual act of worship. Do not conform any longer to the pattern of this world, but be transformed by the renewing of your mind. Then you will be able to test and approve what God's will is—his good, pleasing and perfect will (Romans 12:1-2).

Explore the Word

Read Ephesians 1:3-14.

Successful people have found their place within the Body of Christ. They don't waste their God-given talent on pursuits that counter God's will. They are guided by a clear personal vision of what Christ wants them to accomplish in life—an accurate and precise picture of the work that expresses them best. They have identified their talents and are using them. As a result, these individuals experience profound and lasting benefits: reduced stress, more balance, a more productive career, and a more satisfying life.

Have you anchored your life to the right goal: seeking God's will? If your answer is yes, rest assured that the discipline and commitment you are putting forth is already paying off (even if you don't yet realize it). The more you spend training your spiritual life—reading the Bible, praying, and seeking His guidance—the more God will reveal himself to you.

The fact is, God's will is revealed when we seek Him. God has already mapped out our lives since birth. But it's entirely up to Him when He decides to make His presence and power known directly to us. And once this happens, our lives are forever changed.

LIVE THE WORD

❖ **Steer clear of distractions.** Especially the ones that'll take you down a nowhere track. You know—a lust for money (instead of God's riches), an appetite for immoral sex (instead of the genuine love that Christ offers), a thirst for alcohol and drugs (instead of the joy of pleasing our Creator).

❖ **Get on an eternal track.** Just as an athlete gives his or her all to a sport, Christians need to give the same commitment to God. Once you put God first in your life and trust Him with all your heart, He will show you His power; power that you never imagined. His will for you far surpasses any of your own dreams and goals.

❖ **Keep your balance.** Satan knows exactly the right buttons to push! He sees your weak points and goes after them. But he can't destroy you, that is, if you don't let him. No matter how bad life gets, no matter how much you sin, Jesus still loves you. But it hurts the Lord when you disobey Him. Christ wept for your sin, and He yearns for you to come back to Him. When you blow it, confess your sins to God and ask Him to help you get your life on the right track again.

MY PRAYER:

MY THOUGHTS:

Pride—What's Your Motivation?

"I have to admit that, even after committing my life to Christ, my pride often rears its ugly head. What should I do?"

Examine the Word

Do nothing out of selfish ambition or vain conceit, but in humility consider others better than yourselves. Each of you should look not only to your own interests, but also to the interests of others (Philippians 2:3-4).

Explore the Word

Read Luke 18:9-14.

Pride. Here's a definition worth reviewing: "*(a)* an overhigh opinion of oneself; exaggerated self-esteem; conceit; *(b)* haughty behavior resulting from this; arrogance."

C. S. Lewis describes pride as "spiritual cancer" and warns that its presence in our lives can block us from knowing God: "The essential vice, the utmost evil, is pride. Unchastity, anger, greed, drunkenness, and all that, are mere flea bites in comparison: it was through pride that the devil became the devil: Pride leads to every other vice: it is the complete anti-god state of mind."[3]

Case in point: The Lord warned of judgment for the vain in Isaiah 3:16-17: "The women of Zion are haughty, walking along with outstretched necks, flirting with their eyes. . . . Therefore the Lord will bring sores on the heads of the women of Zion; the LORD will make their scalps bald."

And Christ shocked the Pharisees He was dining with by saying, "For everyone who exalts himself will be humbled, and he who humbles himself will be exalted" (Luke 14:11).

LIVE THE WORD

❖ **Get off the pride ride.** We are often tempted to forget who made us and whose we are. We live in tension. Pride and selfishness struggle desperately to elbow humility and tenderness right out of our lives.

❖ **Ask God to help you get rid of self-promoting, self-seeking, self-satisfied, and just plain selfish attitudes.** As Christians, our role model is God's Son. He didn't wear flashy clothing, give autographs, or even demand to be called "Prince" (though He certainly is). He was a servant of humankind, filled with love and humility. He taught forgiveness, servitude, and trust in God for everything—yet He is the most famous person to ever live.

❖ **Ask Jesus to search your heart.** Pray something like this: "Lord, am I sometimes like the Pharisee that Luke talks about? Do I compare myself with my neighbors, with other members of my church—and seek to convince myself that I'm spiritually superior? Please release me from pride. Amen."

MY PRAYER:

MY THOUGHTS:

Forgiveness—Follow God's Example

"I really messed up. How can Jesus forgive me? I can't even forgive myself."

Examine the Word

The LORD *is compassionate and gracious, slow to anger, abounding in love. He will not always accuse, nor will he harbor his anger forever; he does not treat us as our sins deserve or repay us according to our iniquities* (Psalm 103:8-10).

Explore the Word

Read John 21:15-25.

"Simon," Jesus says in today's Scripture reading, "do you love me more than these?"

You can practically see Peter's mind flashing back to his boastful claim in the Upper Room: "Hey, all these wishy-washy guys may deny You, but not me, no way, no, sirree." That was followed just a few hours later by, "What, are you insane? I've never before laid eyes on this Jesus dude!"

Look closely at this passage. Jesus is not only questioning Peter's devotion but also using the old name Peter had before Jesus changed it. It's as if He's giving Peter a chance to start fresh again.

And Jesus doesn't ask just once. He asks three times. By the third time Peter's heart is breaking. "Lord, You know everything; You know I love You." And for the third time, Jesus commands him to take care of His sheep.

Three times Peter had denied Jesus in the courtyard. And three times Jesus has him confess his loyalty. It is a painful experience, but it is necessary to (1) demonstrate how Christ forgives, and (2) prove to the disciples *and to Peter* that he is back in the group—and that he is once again assigned the task of looking out for others. It will not always be an easy job, but as long as

Peter stays humble and depends on God's power instead of his own ego, he will succeed.

Notice that Christ doesn't clobber us over the head with guilt. He doesn't go around sulking, holding it over our heads or trying to make us feel low. He helps us take responsibility for our sins, then He gently and tenderly tells us that we are forgiven. That's it, end of discussion.

Live the Word

- **Accept God's forgiveness.** When you've blown it in some way, go to the Lord in prayer. Confess your sin, ask for forgiveness, and press ahead with the power of the Lord. Key verse—1 John 1:9: "If we confess our sins, he is faithful and just and will forgive us our sins and purify us from all unrighteousness."
- **Learn from your mistakes.** It's every Christian's responsibility to practice avoiding the traps that cause him or her to stumble. Key verse—Proverbs 26:11: "As a dog returns to its vomit, so a fool repeats his folly."
- **Look to the future.** Keep in mind that God isn't finished with you; the paint's still wet and your faith's still under construction. Growing up in the Lord is a lifetime process. Key verse—Philippians 3:12: "Not that I have already obtained all this, or have already been made perfect, but I press on to take hold of that for which Christ Jesus took hold of me."

My Prayer:

My Thoughts:

Victory Through Christ

"Sometimes I feel as if there's a giant barrier between God and me. Maybe it's my guilty conscience. I have sinned in a number of ways lately—but I just don't know how to talk to Him about it. I feel so weary, so weak."

Examine the Word

So do not throw away your confidence; it will be richly rewarded. You need to persevere so that when you have done the will of God, you will receive what he has promised (Hebrews 10:35-36).

Explore the Word

Read Hebrews 10:19-39.

We're all targets of the evil one. Satan is working overtime to lure us into a hostile position toward God, and he uses every kind of distraction imaginable—boredom, selfish desires, inferiority, drug abuse, doubt, fear, materialism (the list could fill up this book).

Satan's biggest ally is your flesh itself, which is the human, physical dimension of your life that instinctively wants to live independently from God. Even though you now have a new nature in Christ, the sinful world still tempts you to return to those old ways of thinking and living. (See Romans 8:5-8 and Ephesians 2:3.)

So, how can you survive? The answer is basic, but vital—and one you'll find repeated in this book: Have a personal, active relationship with Jesus Christ. The Lord is your ultimate ally, your ultimate defender. You can be victorious through Him.

Live the Word

- **Know the enemy's tactics.** Recognize those areas where you are weakest and most susceptible to Satan's temptations. Then do your best to avoid those areas where you might be tempted to fall.

- **Choose your weapons.** While you can't outsmart or outmuscle the flesh or the devil on your own, you can gain victory in your daily struggle against sin. The Lord has armed every Christian with spiritual weapons packed with "divine power": (1) The sword of the Spirit—the Holy Bible, and (2) prayer. Colossians 3:16 tells Christians to let "the word of Christ richly dwell within you," and Philippians 4:7 promises that "the peace of God . . . shall guard your hearts and your minds in Christ Jesus."

- **Follow your defender.** Merely hanging out at church and "doing your Christian duty" doesn't cut it. You need to know Jesus personally. He is the greatest conqueror ever, and with His guidance, you can have victory against the devil.

My Prayer:

My Thoughts:

Wisdom—Ask for It!

"Time and time again I end up making some pretty dumb choices. How can I wise up?"

Examine the Word

If any of you lacks wisdom, he should ask God, who gives generously to all without finding fault, and it will be given to him. But when he asks, he must believe and not doubt, because he who doubts is like a wave of the sea, blown and tossed by the wind (James 1:5-6).

Explore the Word

Read James 3:13-18.

In his book *Experiencing God,* Henry Blackaby offers some valuable advice that can keep you on the right track: "Through the ages the wisdom found in God's Word has been tested and proven true. It is critical that you measure everything you hear against the Scriptures."[4]

Making wise choices involves more than head knowledge. True wisdom is the ability to apply God's truth to everyday situations. And the wisest action a Christian can take is to admit a wrong he or she has committed, turn to Christ, then start fresh again—in the right direction.

Need wisdom? Study Scripture and pray.

Live the Word

- **Plug in to the Word.** You'll hear all kinds of reasons why some people favor their feelings over the Bible: "It was written too long ago to really be relevant today." "It just doesn't make any sense to me." "No one can know for sure that it's 100 percent accurate."

  Despite some people's doubts, God's Word is timeless and absolutely, positively accurate in everything He felt was essential for us to know. While there is room for debate on irrelevant issues (like whether Judas hanged himself or whether he stabbed himself), there are no discrepancies in His promises, commands, and warnings. And the fact is, archaeologists and researchers are constantly making new discoveries that confirm the Bible's authority.

- **Don't neglect prayer.** Jesus Christ himself made prayer a priority. He "went out to the mountainside to pray, and spent the night praying to God" (Luke 6:12). He demonstrated for us that daily communication is central to a personal relationship with our Heavenly Father. He even told His disciples a parable "to show them that they should always pray and not give up" (Luke 18:1).

MY PRAYER:

MY THOUGHTS:

Meditation–Sharpen Your Focus

"When the Bible instructs us to meditate on Scripture or a faith lesson, what exactly does that mean?"

Examine the Word

I will remember the deeds of the L*ORD; yes, I will remember your miracles of long ago. I will meditate on all your works and consider all your mighty deeds* (Psalm 77:11-12).

Explore the Word

Read Psalm 19.

Do you remember when you first became a Christian? As it is with most people, that unforgettable experience was probably a little like a roller-coaster ride.

First, you felt a rush of excitement and enthusiasm . . . and couldn't wait to tell the world about your new relationship with Jesus. Then, a few months down the road, you hit bottom and the zeal seemed to fade. When you were around your peers at school or work, you may have caught yourself feeling a bit embarrassed about what you believed.

You couldn't help scratching your head and wondering, *Exactly WHAT happened?*

Hopefully, a warning from 1 Thessalonians 5:19 rang in your ears: *"Do not put out the Spirit's fire."* And, hopefully, you soon learned that your "faith fire" was fizzling.

Why? Because you probably weren't fueling it. More than likely, you weren't spending time reading the Word, savoring and studying Scripture (Examine the Word), meditating upon it and soaking it in (Explore the Word) . . . and applying it to your life (Live the Word). No doubt, when your convictions were on the line and the pressure hit hard, you probably didn't have the strength to stand firm.

As you continue to grow in your faith, you'll develop a greater desire to slow down and take the time to digest—or meditate upon—Scripture. Here's an idea: during your quiet times, ask God to be your Teacher. After all, the Scriptures have been inspired by the Lord. Expect that each day the Holy Spirit will bring you a sense of God's presence in His Word.

Live the Word

- **Meditate on the Word daily.** Commit right now to setting aside a portion of your day (at least five days a week) studying a few passages from the Bible—along with daily readings from a devotional guide like this one.
- **Learn the sword-fighting basics.** (1) Pray before you read Scripture. Ask the Holy Spirit to illuminate your mind and to help you understand the scriptural truths you'll encounter. (2) Don't attempt to read the Bible as you would a school textbook, racing through big blocks of type. The Holy Scriptures are unlike anything else you'll ever study. Every word is inspired by God and is like a collection of personal letters written by our Heavenly Father just for us. Savor each word, rereading passages, chewing on them, meditating on each verse.
- **Carry your sword into battle.** God's holy words can empower your life if you do two things: memorize and apply. As you read through the Bible each day, highlight a passage or two and begin committing them to memory.

My Prayer:

My Thoughts:

Day 15

Commitment—Pressing On

"What's the key to being all that God wants me to be?"

Examine the Word

For the eyes of the LORD *range throughout the earth to strengthen those whose hearts are fully committed to him* (2 Chronicles 16:9).

Explore the Word

Read Deuteronomy 31:1-8.

It's a grueling journey, and the fleet of 11 ships is battered almost beyond repair. Even harder hit are the nerves of the crew.

"Has our captain gone mad?!" yells a sailor.

"He'll end up getting us all killed," complains another.

"I say we turn around and GO BACK!" insists a crewman.

Suddenly, fear erupts on the decks. "GO BACK! GO BACK! GO BACK! Let's go back to the life we once knew."

But Hernán Cortés won't budge. He has amassed his battalion of 508 soldiers and 100 sailors and has set out on an important mission for the king of Spain: Explore the New World.

Cortés silences the crowd. "Gentlemen, we can't go back now. This is our destiny. We were made for this moment."

Then he reminds his men of the words he had printed on a banner: "Brothers and comrades, let us follow the sign of the Holy Cross in true faith, for under this sign we shall conquer."

It works. And soon the ships reach Mexico.

Yet Cortés doesn't let out a sigh of relief. He knows other storms are just on the horizon. So he quickly goes to work, disciplining his army, welding it into a cohesive force.

Then the famous conquistador does something that will be retold again and again in the history books: He orders his men to burn the ships.

By doing so, Cortés actually saves the lives of his crew. Since the ships are so weather-beaten from the journey, returning to Spain would be risky. And by that single action, Cortés commits himself and his entire force to survival through conquest. It also ensures that they keep their eyes on the New World, not on the life they left behind.

As Christians, Jesus has called us to burn our ship too.

Following Him involves a lifetime commitment. We have come to a whole new world through our relationship with Christ—and there's no turning back. But nobody said it would be easy (not even Christ).

Do you sometimes have doubts about the Lord's power in your life? (Are you sometimes a chameleon for Christ—a member of God's Secret Service?) If so, it's time to "burn a ship or two."

It's God's plan that we move toward the goal of becoming more like His Son, Jesus Christ. This is a big goal; that's why God gave us a lifetime to work on it. But it all begins by burning the ships and keeping your eyes on the New World, not on the life you left behind.

Live the Word

- **Follow the compass.** Jesus knows there will be hardships and times when we wish we could go back to "safer" ground. Remember that He is there for you. He'll help you through the tough times. He won't sit idly by, hoping you'll have the strength to withstand. He wants to provide the inner muscle it takes to combat the outer pressure you feel.

- **Stay on course.** Jesus wants you to be a person of depth. He doesn't want you to sell out for what's comfortable or go back to the old life you once knew. He's calling you to plug in to His power through prayer and Bible study . . . and set your sights on a greater world ahead.

- **Drop anchor.** As a Christian, you are expected to be a defender. How? By living a life with conscience. The next time you're in a tight spot, ask yourself this question: *Am I willing to throw away what's right and settle for stuff that's wrong (just to please the crowd)?*

MY PRAYER:

MY THOUGHTS:

Day 16

Jesus Christ—the Source of All Hope

"Where can I find hope in this hopeless world?"

Examine the Word

We have this hope as an anchor for the soul, firm and secure. It enters the inner sanctuary behind the curtain, where Jesus, who went before us, has entered on our behalf. He has become a high priest forever, in the order of Melchizedek (Hebrews 6:19).

Explore the Word

Read Genesis 3:1-24.

Today's Scripture reading chronicles the beginning of misery—and hope. The story moves from sin and evil to shame and cover-up, broken fellowship, erected barriers, attack on God, flight from God. It's the story of the Fall, out of which C. S. Lewis says "has come nearly all that we call human history—money, poverty, ambition, war, prostitution, classes, empire, slavery—the long terrible story of man trying to find something other than God that will make him happy."

Yet the story of the Fall is also one of grace—God's grace—and hope. It's the hope that began when God broke our unholy alliance with the devil and removed hostility between Him and us. Misery is still with us. But the time is getting shorter, and the hope is getting brighter.[5]

❖ For Christ died for sins once for all, the righteous for the unrighteous, to bring you to God" (1 Peter 3:18).

❖ For God so loved the world that he gave his one and only Son, that whoever believes in him shall not perish but have eternal life" (John 3:16).

Through Jesus Christ, your sins are completely forgiven. Your slate is clean. You have a spotless record with Him and can now have eternal fellowship with God. Through Jesus Christ, humanity's misery turns to eternal hope!

Live the Word

- **God did not leave you as an orphan.** In times of distress call out to God, and He will give you the power of the Holy Spirit. "Again Jesus said, 'Peace be with you! As the Father has sent me, I am sending you.' And with that he breathed on them and said, 'Receive the Holy Spirit' " (John 20:21-22).
- **Cling to the truth that we can handle whatever it is that God expects of us.** "This is love for God: to obey his commands. And his commands are not burdensome, for everyone born of God overcomes the world" (1 John 5:3-4).

My Prayer:

My Thoughts:

Day 17

Bitterness—Examine Your Heart

"How can I release the bitterness in my heart?"

Examine the Word

Get rid of all bitterness, rage and anger, brawling and slander, along with every form of malice. Be kind and compassionate to one another, forgiving each other, just as in Christ God forgave you (Ephesians 4:31-32).

Explore the Word

Read 1 Timothy 2:1-8.

In today's Scripture reading, Paul lets us in on a key to overcoming bitterness: If we thank God for other people—even our enemies—we will "live peaceful and quiet lives" (1 Timothy 2:2).

What's that? you say. *Pray for my enemies—impossible!*

Give it a try. Something amazing—something supernatural—just may happen in your life. You see, when we pray for someone, we enter into that person's life. (They become less of a monster and more human to us.) What's more, when we are angry and full of bitterness, we are usually wrapped up in ourselves. But when we pray for the needs of others, our own troubles often fade into the background—allowing peace to fill our lives.

Live the Word

- **Steer clear of a "bitterness burn."** Bitterness hurts you far more than it hurts others. Here's how one pastor described the danger of an unforgiving heart: "It's like a hot coal. The longer and tighter it is held, the deeper the burn. Like a hot coal, bitterness, too, will leave a scar that even time cannot erase."

❖ **Forgive—then forgive again.** Think of all the ways you may have been wronged by someone, then work toward genuine forgiveness. But, first, understand that forgiveness is not: *(a)* denying that you've been hurt; *(b)* explaining away the wrong action someone has brought against you; or *(c)* trying to understand why a person has acted a certain way. Genuine forgiveness involves consciously choosing to release the hurt someone has caused—and continuing to love that person.

MY PRAYER:

MY THOUGHTS:

Day 18

Find True Fulfillment in Faith

"As I read Bible stories about Jesus and His life in the Holy Land, I find it ironic that, today, Jerusalem is a chaotic and sometimes dangerous place. Why is that?"

Examine the Word

The LORD is near to all who call on him, to all who call on him in truth. He fulfills the desires of those who fear him; he hears their cry and saves them (Psalm 145:18-19).

Explore the Word

Read Acts 1:1-11.

Jerusalem is truly the "crossroads of life." It's the place where you can walk in the footsteps of Jesus and, at the same time, witness a chaotic culture that's torn apart by political and religious disagreements. (A culture that often values man's rules over God's.) Yet as a people, those who live in the Holy Land represent all of humanity.

As you soak in Israel's many ancient sights, you can't help being reminded of an awesome truth: while the glory of this world is fleeting and flawed by strife, true fulfillment can be found by knowing intimately, loving intensely, serving passionately, and trusting completely Jesus Christ. Eternal peace is at the core of God's gift of salvation.

A restored Israel is very close to the heart of God. It's the restoration not only of a people to a land but of all people to their God. This is where true fulfillment can be found. This is what we all should be seeking.

Live the Word

❖ **Don't look to the world for true fulfillment—look to God.** Isn't it ironic that the "Holy Land" is one of the most chaotic regions of the world? Understand this: strong forces, based on ancient religious beliefs, are at work in the Arab-Israeli struggle. Yet there is hope even today for the troubled Middle East, as well as the entire world. Every one of Abraham's children—Arab, Jew, and Gentile alike—has the same opportunity of receiving God's gift of eternal life, offered in His chosen Messiah.

❖ **Love Christ FIRST.** Scripture reminds us to focus on the Lord, and to recognize that Christians have the key to a significant, marvelous, joyful, and fulfilling life. It's all grounded on a relationship with Jesus Christ. Get to know the voice of the Lord as clearly as you are able. Strengthen your relationship with Him *first*, then devote your energy to the other relationships in your life.

MY PRAYER:

MY THOUGHTS:

Why Pray?

"God is God, and He knows everything—our past, present, and future. So, why do we need to pray?"

Examine the Word

Devote yourselves to prayer, being watchful and thankful. And pray for us, too, that God may open a door for our message, so that we may proclaim the mystery of Christ, for which I am in chains. Pray that I may proclaim it clearly, as I should. Be wise in the way you act toward outsiders; make the most of every opportunity. Let your conversation be always full of grace, seasoned with salt, so that you may know how to answer everyone (Colossians 4:2-6).

Explore the Word

Read 1 Thessalonians 5:12-28.

Paul was serious when he wrote, "Pray continually" (1 Thessalonians 5:17). Jesus wants you conversing with Him all day long. Consider these thoughts about prayer:

- ❖ You don't need to be in church.
- ❖ You don't need to kneel.
- ❖ You don't need to do anything with your hands.
- ❖ You don't even have to raise your voice.

So, why pray? C. S. Lewis has an answer. In his book *The Efficacy of Prayer,* he suggests that God doesn't really need us to help Him do what He does. After all, God is the one with infinite wisdom and goodness. What can we who are far from perfect have to offer God? However, Lewis goes on to suggest that while God doesn't *need* us to make things happen, He still *wants* to connect with us because He loves us so much.

In other words, the reason God wants us to pray is as simple as it is profound and awe-inspiring: the Lord wants to involve us in the "process." As Pascal said (quoted by Lewis in the same essay), "God instituted prayer in order to lend to His creatures the dignity of causality." God in His infinite wisdom has chosen to grant us the honor of participating in His works.

LIVE THE WORD

- **God's ever-giving heart allows us to approach Him.** "Your voice matters in heaven," writes author Max Lucado. "He takes you very seriously. When you enter His presence, He turns to you to hear your voice. No need to fear that you will be ignored."[6]
- **Pray continually.** Strive to make Christ your first thought in the morning, your constant companion throughout the day, the One you imitate in public, and your last thought at night. Consider what He wants for your life, and place it above your personal desires.

MY PRAYER:

MY THOUGHTS:

Prayer Is Communication with God

"If prayer is how we communicate with God, does He ever speak to us in an audible voice?"

Examine the Word

The eyes of the Lord are on the righteous and his ears are attentive to their cry (Psalm 34:15).

Explore the Word

Read Jude 17-25.

Prayer is powerful. It's not just saying a few words or making a bunch of requests—it's intimate communication with our eternal God. Imagine that! The Creator of the universe welcomes us into His presence. He even delights in it!

When you have a close relationship with Jesus, He will tell you what He wants you to do. He communicates with you throughout the day, answering your questions and guiding your steps. You literally walk in His presence minute by minute.

Since prayer is communication, does God talk to people with an audible voice? Let's clear up this misconception once and for all. The answer: not usually. In fact, He rarely communicates with most of us this way, if ever. Instead, the Holy Spirit deals with each human being in a personal and intimate way, convicting, directing, and influencing us.

God has promised to speak to our hearts, so we can expect Him to, but He is not compelled to tell us everything we want to know the moment we desire the information. Therefore, it's important that we nurture a consistent, growing relationship with Him.

LIVE THE WORD

❖ **Be still and listen.** After you've spent time talking to God in prayer, spend some time listening to Him. This means doing nothing. Tune into your conscience. Give God a chance to speak to your heart.

❖ **Tune into the spiritual discernment the Holy Spirit provides.** This awareness takes on a "something's not quite right" feeling when God is trying to get you to avoid a course of action—or when danger is lurking nearby. On the other hand, peace and a sense of confidence are the signs of spiritual awareness that God gives when you're on the right track. And as you grow closer and closer to Him, your instincts will become more sensitive to His influence. Your entire mind and spirit will become more in tune to God, and you'll begin to hear Him more clearly, just as with any good friend.

MY PRAYER:

MY THOUGHTS:

How to Pray

"I hear so much about the importance of prayer, yet I don't know how to do it. I close my eyes and begin talking to God. But I can't help wondering, *Is God listening? Am I doing this right?*"

Examine the Word

One day Jesus was praying in a certain place. When he finished, one of his disciples said to him, "Lord, teach us to pray, just as John taught his disciples" (Luke 11:1).

Explore the Word

Read Matthew 6:5-13.

Even though Christ's disciples had prayed with Jesus many times and in many different places, the Lord had never instructed them on how to pray or on what to say. So the inevitable question was asked: "Lord, teach us to pray" (Luke 11:1).

Jesus was probably thrilled by their willingness to learn. Let's listen in on His instruction (based on Matthew 6:5-13):

"Don't shout on a street corner as some people do. That's the first thing.

"Don't pray in a crowd. It's better to pray alone.

"Remember, God knows what you need before you ask, but he wants you to ask anyway."

"What's the best prayer?" asked Peter.

"Would you like to know my favorite prayer?" Jesus asked.

"Here's how you should pray: 'Our Father which art in heaven, Hallowed be thy name. Thy kingdom come. Thy will be done in earth, as it is in heaven.

" 'Give us this day our daily bread. And forgive us our debts as we forgive our debtors. And lead us not into temptation, but deliver us from evil: For thine is the kingdom, and the power, and the glory, for ever. Amen' " (KJV).

Even today, too many Christians neglect prayer. Either they don't know how to do it, or they haven't fully grasped the importance of this important activity. In today's Scripture reading, Jesus gives us an example to follow. Christ shows us that prayer is a gift from the Lord and the work of the Holy Spirit. It's the key to being empowered as well as a skill we must develop for successful Christian living.

Prayer is an essential part of every believer's life. Have you made it a priority in your life? You can't use the excuse that you don't know how.

Live the Word

- **Stop procrastinating and pray!** There are lots of people who advocate formulas on proper prayer techniques. Some even insist that real prayer happens only during certain times of the day. But here's the truth: prayer is based on a personal relationship with Jesus Christ. There are no ideal words or established formats. We can pray anytime, anywhere.
- **Pray about anything.** You've figured out how to talk to a friend on the phone or how to send E-mail—so prayer should be easy, too. Jesus is your best friend, and He wants you to tell Him about everything that's going on in your life. He wants to know the desires of your heart, how badly you feel when you fail, how happy you are when good things happen—anything! But as we learned from today's scripture passage, Jesus doesn't want you to make prayer mindless babble or nothing more than a show to impress others. He wants it to be intimate and sincere.

MY PRAYER:

MY THOUGHTS:

Christ's Prayer Life

"I'm tired of going through the motions. I want my prayer life to be powerful and effective. What should I do?"

Examine the Word

Very early in the morning, while it was still dark, Jesus got up, left the house and went off to a solitary place, where he prayed (Mark 1:35).

Explore the Word

Read John 17:1-19.

Probably no other section of Scripture more accurately captures the heart and deepest desires of Jesus than this prayer. For the first time, He lets the disciples (and us) eavesdrop on His most intimate conversation with His Father.

Jesus prays for himself. First He asks to be glorified "with the glory I had with you before the world began" (v. 5). Jesus is not on some power trip here. He knows that He is about to face more agony than any human being has ever faced in the history of the world—not just the pain of the Cross, mind you, but the suffering and punishment for all the world's sins. For those few hours He'll literally be carrying the weight of the entire world on His shoulders.

And He knows one other thing—He knows He can back out and call it quits any time He wants.

So He's praying for the strength and courage to go through with it, to succeed. If He does, there is no more perfect demonstration of God's love for us—or of His Son's immense glory.

Jesus prays for the disciples. Next, He begins praying for His friends. First, He asks for unity. It's as if He already knows the centuries of arguments and fights that are going to plague the church—everything from wars over major doctrines to hurt feelings about what color the curtains in the church bathroom should be.

Then He prays that even though the world may hate them, His followers will have the "full measure" of His joy. Again Jesus makes it clear that real joy doesn't necessarily depend on outward circumstances. Real joy comes from the depth of our relationship with God.

Jesus prays for protection. Finally, He asks the Father to protect the disciples from the world. *Not to take them out of the world*—but to protect them while they're in it.[7]

Want your prayer life to be effective? Follow Christ's example.

Live the Word

- **Go off to a lonely place and pray.** Find a private place—*anywhere:* your bedroom, the kitchen table while everyone else is asleep, an undisturbed corner of your school's library—and carve out a block of "quiet time" every day for prayer. Exactly what time you do this and for how long is up to you.
- **Make sure you're alone with God.** The key is to have some time alone with God so that you can give Him your undivided attention. A committed, unhurried quiet time is actually the most important part of a Christian's day.

My Prayer:

My Thoughts:

Day 23

Praise and Prayer

"I'm bored with church—and catch myself wondering if Christianity really makes a difference in my life. How can I give my spiritual passion a much-needed zap?"

Examine the Word

Praise the **LORD**. *Praise the name of the* **LORD**; *praise him, you servants of the* **LORD**, *you who minister in the house of the* **LORD**, *in the courts of the house of our God. Praise the* **LORD**, *for the* **LORD** *is good; sing praise to his name, for that is pleasant* (Psalm 135:1-3).

Explore the Word

Read John 21:1-14.

Today's Scripture reading captures a snapshot of high-voltage JOY! What began as a pretty gloomy day turned into a loud, rip-roaring celebration—and Jesus was at the center of it all!

The scene begins the morning after what Peter would no doubt call "The Worst Day of My Life!" That would be the day his friend—the man he called "teacher" for so long, yet who he turned his back on—was nailed to a cross.

Peter and his buddies were hanging out in a boat on the Sea of Tiberias—doing their best to get on with their lives as fishermen. Then it happened.

"Friends, haven't you any fish?" a guy called out to them.

Peter looked up from the water and spotted a guy kneeling alone on the shore, trying to start a campfire. "No," Peter answered.

"Throw your net on the right side of the boat, and you will find some."

What—is this guy crazy? Peter probably wondered. The last thing he needed was some landlubber telling him how to fish. Yet his voice seemed strangely familiar. And when the guys did as the man said, something amazing happened: they were unable to haul the net in because of the large number of fish.

John was the first to recognize the stranger. And as soon as he let Peter know, old Pete cannonballed into the water (clothes and all), leaving the rest of the guys to fight with the fish. That guy on the shore was no stranger. He was their buddy . . . their teacher . . . their LORD! Everything else paled by comparison.

A catch of 153 large fish was something worth celebrating. But most important of all, their friend who was hanging on a cross just days earlier and then placed into a dark tomb was alive! He defeated death! Jesus truly was who He claimed to be—our Lord and Savior.

What started as the worst day of Peter's life became the first day of his *eternal life*. The whole world had much to celebrate! Our Savior is with us. God is victorious!

Live the Word

- **How is praising God an important part of prayer?** Are worship times supposed to be silent and serious . . . or loud and jubilant? (Is it possible that praising Jesus can be both—noisy and quiet?)
- **Are your quiet times dry?** Does Jesus seem distant? Do business with the Lord right now—don't delay. Tell Him what's bugging you. Share your doubts, fears, frustrations, and your failures. Ask Jesus to do the miraculous in your life.
- **Stop and take the time to praise Jesus right now.** It's easy to praise God when everything is going our way. But what about life's tough times? Is it possible to praise God when bad things happen?

MY PRAYER:

MY THOUGHTS:

Pray and Repent

"I'm trapped in sin. I try to stop doing what I know is wrong, but it's as if I have no control. What should I do?"

Examine the Word

Is any one of you in trouble? He should pray. Is anyone happy? Let him sing songs of praise. Is any one of you sick? He should call the elders of the church to pray over him and anoint him with oil in the name of the Lord. And the prayer offered in faith will make the sick person well; the Lord will raise him up. If he has sinned, he will be forgiven. Therefore confess your sins to each other and pray for each other so that you may be healed. The prayer of a righteous man is powerful and effective (James 5:13-16).

Explore the Word

Read Romans 7:7-25.

"For what I do is not the good I want to do; no, the evil I do not want to do—this I keep on doing. Now if I do what I do not want to do, it is no longer I who do it, but it is sin living in me that does it" (Romans 7:19-20).

Can you identify with Paul's agony? Even though you've asked Christ into your heart, your old sinful nature still exists. And if you give it a chance by encouraging it, it literally takes control. The result: a strained relationship with God.

So, how can you make things right again? How can you keep your old nature from ruining your new life? If you made it to the end of today's Scripture reading, then you know Paul discovered the answer: Jesus Christ. (And Paul gives more hope in chapter 8.)

Go to Him in prayer and confess your sins. Tell Him all about your struggles, and tell Him you're sorry. He'll forgive you. "If we confess our sins, he is faithful and just and will forgive us our sins and purify us from all unrighteousness" (1 John 1:9).

Confess your need to God and surrender yourself to His will. When you do this, God fills you with His Holy Spirit. God cleanses the sinful nature (original sin) from your heart. The Holy Spirit then gives you power to live for and serve God. This is the act of entire sanctification—you surrender yourself to God, and He sanctifies you.

What's the result of this entire sanctification? When God cleanses the sinful nature, He removes the desire to sin. He makes the person's heart pure and holy. The person receives power to serve God with all of his or her heart and to witness. Prior to this experience, most people do not understand or have access to the power and the joy that the Holy Spirit brings.

Ask Jesus to go deep in your heart and to heal the *real* cause of what's making you stumble. Very often the *real* problem usually isn't what a person thinks it is. Struggles with drugs or lust are almost always just the symptoms. The *real problem* is actually *a heart problem.* And the only way to fix a mixed-up, sin-filled heart is by having a daily truth encounter. That means *spending time in the Word and in prayer.*

Combine Bible reading with prayer and you've got a powerful weapon—an invisible sword, so to speak—that can fend off any deception and defeat ANY struggle that threatens to trap us.

Live the Word

- **Give up the performance trap.** Following the "letter of the law" and trying to be "a good person" won't bring you life.
- **Stop reliving old sins.** And stop thinking that you just can't cut it as a Christian. Get this truth through your head: If you've confessed your sins to Jesus and have committed your life to Him, you are forgiven and free! Not only free from punishment, but if you let Him, He can actually free you from sinning!

MY PRAYER:

MY THOUGHTS:

How to "Ask" Through Prayer

"Is it true that I can ask God for anything?"

Examine the Word

"So I say to you: Ask and it will be given to you; seek and you will find; knock and the door will be opened to you. For everyone who asks receives; he who seeks finds; and to him who knocks, the door will be opened" (Luke 11:9-10).

Explore the Word

Read Mark 1:40-45.

Broken. Lonely. Desperate.

The outcast spends his life on the fringes, and his days lived in the shadows. But news travels quickly throughout Galilee—even these forgotten back roads.

The man knows he doesn't have a minute to waste. This is his only hope. He must reach the center of town. Not making it there means destruction. The eternal end to an already pitiful life.

The man covers his hideous physique in a smelly wrap and steps out of a dark alley. Suddenly, a scream. The man peeks out his hood and watches as a woman grabs a child and races to the other side of the street.

"Don't come around here," yells a person on his right.

"Stay away," screams another. "You know you're NOT welcome!"

"Get away from us, you unclean man . . . you LEPER."

Everywhere he goes, the man faces rejection. But that doesn't stop him. He ignores the painful words and continues to hobble along the hot, dusty road—eventually reaching a crowd at the end of the way.

Standing among the people is the only man who won't reject him—a man who has the power to make him well.

Right there, in the middle of the crowd, is the most famous Person on earth. A Nazarene. A carpenter. God in the flesh.

Right there—speaking to the broken, the lonely, the desperate—is a man named Jesus.

And when the leper reaches Jesus, a most incredible thing happens. The leper falls on his knees and begs, "If you are willing, you can make me clean."

Filled with compassion, Jesus reaches out His hand and touches the man. "I am willing," Jesus says. "Be clean!" And immediately the leprosy leaves the man, and the man is cured.

Amazing story. You see, the leper wasn't just some no-name person who got a second chance at life. This outcast represents you and me. His repulsive, deadly disease symbolizes a malady that plagues us all. Oh, sure, we may not have a scarred outer appearance, but we are scarred on the inside. We all have a condition called sin.

When the Great Physician reached out His hand and said, "I am willing," He was talking to you and me.

If we seek out the Savior and ask, He is willing and able and faithful. So, what's holding you back?

Live the Word

- **God is the Supreme Giver.** Take a look at these thoughts from Pastor Charles Stanley: "We have life only because God has created us by an exercise of His will. We can receive salvation only because He wills to grant it."[8]
- **Know where you are headed.** Where is your life right now? Are you still crawling . . . and clawing . . . and inching your way through life? Do you feel like a shell of a teen that's just wasting away? Are you facing major rejection everywhere you turn? Don't let that stop you. Jesus is right here today—stretching out His hand to you. Take it. He's offering you freedom, and forgiveness . . . and a whole new life with Him.

MY PRAYER:

MY THOUGHTS:

Surrender All Through Prayer

"What's the secret to being radically committed to God?"

Examine the Word

"If anyone would come after me, he must deny himself and take up his cross daily and follow me. For whoever wants to save his life will lose it, but whoever loses his life for me will save it" (Luke 9:23-24).

Explore the Word

Read Luke 9:18-27.

Who or what is the passion of your life? Being radically committed to Jesus means allowing Him to consume your life. It means carrying the cross of Christ daily.

The Lord doesn't ask us to add a little of himself into our daily walk—He asks to *become* our lives. He's not interested in people who dabble in a relationship with Him, He's interested in people who *live* Him—faithfully, consistently, day by day.

Revelation 3:15-16 says, "I know your deeds, that you are neither cold nor hot. I wish you were either one or the other! So, because you are lukewarm—neither hot nor cold—I am about to spit you out of my mouth."

The point is this: Jesus is not interested in people who play church. He's interested in people who are the Church—people who are a living, breathing, loving part of His Body—people who are totally committed to Him. What's more, God loves us too much to "leave us in diapers." He wants us to grow up—mentally, physically, spiritually, and socially—just like His Son (Luke 2:52).

LIVE THE WORD

- **Do you truly want to make knowing, serving, loving, and communicating God your number one passion?** Or are you more like the multitudes described in the New Testament—people who were just hanging around Jesus for another free meal, or because that's where their friends were, or because they wanted to use Jesus for selfish motives?

- **Commit to the worship of God, the work of God, and the Word of God.** The most successful people in any field are those who are totally committed to what they believe. Are you committed to being a Christian—to following Jesus?

MY PRAYER:

MY THOUGHTS:

The Courage to Pray

"Sometimes it's easier just to blend in than to stand up for my faith. Pray in public? I'm not sure if I can do that! How can I have more courage?"

Examine the Word

"My God sent his angel, and he shut the mouths of the lions. They have not hurt me, because I was found innocent in his sight" (Daniel 6:22).

Explore the Word

Read Daniel 6:1-28.

Obedience to God. Radical, unwavering submission to the one, true King—even at the risk of losing popularity, prestige, position. Even in the deadly grip of a lion's fangs.

Daniel knows this degree of obedience, and despite the order not to pray, he stays committed to God. After all, he's seen the Master's hand move in amazing ways—especially the time when three fellow believers were thrown into a blazing furnace.

The flames were so hot that King Nebuchadnezzar's soldiers died as they threw Shadrach, Meshach, and Abednego into the fire. Yet the men of God stepped out of the furnace unharmed. Not a single hair on their heads was singed!

"Praise be to the God of Shadrach, Meshach and Abednego," Nebuchadnezzar proclaimed. "They trusted in him and defied the king's command and were willing to give up their lives rather than serve or worship any god except their own God."

But can the hardhearted people of this world ever learn? Now, many years later, the opposition to God and His people continues. This time, Babylon's administrators have convinced the new king, Darius the Mede, to issue an unjust decree: "Anyone who prays to any god or man during the next thirty days, except to you, O king, shall be thrown into the lions' den."

Daniel doesn't flinch. He kneels at his upstairs window—the one opened toward Jerusalem—and prays three times a day, giving thanks to God . . . just as always.

"Did you not publish a decree?" the administrators ask the king.

"The decree stands," the ruler replies, and Daniel is quickly thrown into the lions' den.

"May your God, whom you serve continually, rescue you," the king tells Daniel. Then a stone is placed over the mouth of the den.

Will Daniel's life end with the fierce swipe of a lion's paw? Not a chance! Just as with the miracle in the furnace, God protects and prospers His obedient children.

Daniel emerges unscratched, and King Darius is overjoyed: "For he is the living God and he endures forever. . . . He rescues and he saves; he performs signs and wonders in the heavens and on the earth. He has rescued Daniel from the power of the lions."

Radical obedience. Unwavering submission to the King of Kings. That's how Daniel lived his faith. He didn't know exactly what would happen to him in the pit of the lions' den, but he did know this: God is God, the one and only God, and He can be trusted—even when a dozen lions are poised to pounce.

Do your decisions honor God and speak boldly of your obedience to Him?

Live the Word

- ❖ **Count the cost.** Living for Christ is expensive—it costs everything! (Especially stuff like trust, commitment, and 100-percent, rock-solid obedience to Him.) The choice is yours. Will you follow the crowd and conform to the world, or, like Daniel, commit yourself to standing strong for God (and maybe even leading your friends in a radical eternal direction)? It all starts with the first step: desire to follow Christ.
- ❖ **Remove the roadblocks . . .** this is the next crucial step. Ask Jesus to search your heart and to help you pinpoint specific sins that are holding you back from an obedient relationship with Him. After praying, take out a notebook and a pen. On the top left-hand side of one page write: "Things I Must Get Right with God." Then list all the stuff you need to confess to the Lord. Ask God to do a deep work in your soul. Allow Him to examine every area of your life. (Example: Perhaps you have a problem with envy or a bad temper. Confess these to God.)

MY PRAYER:

MY THOUGHTS:

Day 28

One Body, Many Parts

"How can I find my spiritual gifts and talents?"

Examine the Word

The body is a unit, though it is made up of many parts; and though all its parts are many, they form one body. So it is with Christ. . . . Now you are the body of Christ, and each one of you is a part of it (1 Corinthians 12:12, 27).

Explore the Word

Read 1 Corinthians 12:12-31.

The apostle Paul tells us that we are all part of the Body of Christ, called the Church. Though there are many members of the Body, there is still one Body, one cause, one Creator we serve.

While God bestows an amazing array of gifts upon His creation, each member has been chosen by Him to make a unique contribution to the Body. In other words, the Body *needs* each member, and each member *needs* the Body. And each member is called to be loyal to her Head, to his Master—to fulfill His purpose for their lives, to perform the functions that keep the Body vibrantly alive and in step with the living Head, our Lord Jesus Christ.

So, what's the key to discovering your spiritual gifts? You'll find your unique place in this world—and, ultimately, true fulfillment—if you *fit yourself into what God wants for you rather than what you want for yourself.*

LIVE THE WORD

- **Pick a profession that's in tune with God's will for your life.** How? Take your dreams and desires to God, and trust Him with the outcome. Is the Lord directing your steps? If so, Proverbs 16:3 promises that you're on the right track: "Commit to the Lord whatever you do, and your plans will succeed." But keep in mind that your plans have no strength if they're not from God.
- **Consider the gifts and talents God has given you.** Ask God to reveal what His good, pleasing, and perfect will looks like for you (Romans 12:2).
- **Pursue what is kind, just, and loving even if you don't make as much money:** "Better a little with righteousness than much gain with injustice" (Proverbs 16:8).

MY PRAYER:

MY THOUGHTS:

Day 29

Walk with Integrity

"How do Christians define *integrity*, and how are we supposed to 'live it' in the world?"

Examine the Word

For no one can lay any foundation other than the one already laid, which is Jesus Christ. If any man builds on this foundation using gold, silver, costly stones, wood, hay or straw, his work will be shown for what it is, because the Day will bring it to light. It will be revealed with fire, and the fire will test the quality of each man's work. If what he has built is burned up, he will suffer loss; he himself will be saved, but only as one escaping through the flames (1 Corinthians 3:11-15).

Explore the Word

Read John 19:1-16.

First, Jesus is flogged by a whip with multiple leather strips—each strip having a sharp, jagged piece of stone or metal tied at its end to make sure it digs nice and deep into the flesh.

Next, His captors weave a crown of thorns and jam it down hard on His head. And by thorns we're not talking your standard blackberry or rose variety. We're talking about a plant in that region whose thorns are about an inch long and as sharp as sewing needles.

They wrap a robe around His body, which by now looks like one big, open wound. Later, when the blood has dried to it, they'll rip it off.

As a final insult, they begin spitting on Him and beating Him. In fact, the soldiers get to playing a little game with Him, demanding that Jesus prophesy who will hit Him next as they punch Him in the face again and again and again.

Meanwhile, Pilate pleads with the religious officials, "This man is innocent. Let Him go!"

Their response: "Crucify Him!"

Despite unspeakable cruelty by evil men, Jesus didn't snap. When the pressure intensified, Christ stood strong. He lived His integrity all the way to the Cross.

As the Scriptures tell us, the rewards for following His example on earth last forever in heaven. The fact is, we simply don't have much of a future without integrity. Proverbs 10:9 describes it this way: "The man of integrity walks securely."

Here are some other clues the Bible gives us about integrity:

- Integrity serves as a guide in life's moral decisions (Proverbs 11:3).
- Integrity hates falsehood in every form (Proverbs 13:5-6).
- Integrity is something to be held onto, even in tough times (Job 2:3).
- Integrity keeps its word even when it hurts (Psalm 15:1-4).
- Integrity isn't afraid to run when evil comes knocking (2 Timothy 2:22).
- Integrity means what it says (James 5:12).
- Integrity backs up what it says with how it lives (Titus 2:7).
- Integrity is what God looks for in a person's character (1 Chronicles 29:17).

Live the Word

- **Integrity happens one choice at a time.** Your initial decision not to cross a certain line will plant the seed. "I will not cheat" is a decision that places the acorn of integrity in the soil of your heart. But it doesn't stop there. You've got to water it, nurture it, help it to grow. Every time you keep a promise, even though it may come at a high cost, your integrity is watered. Every time you choose to tell the truth when tempted to lie, you strengthen your integrity.
- **Strive to consistently walk your talk.** Integrity is about reputation. It's not a hidden characteristic. It's a public thing. Make sure you live out what you say you believe.

MY PRAYER:

MY THOUGHTS:

Day 30

Standing Up to Persecution

"I want to be a committed Christian, but the thought of being persecuted for my faith scares me. How can I handle hard times when they hit?"

Examine the Word

"For I will give you words and wisdom that none of your adversaries will be able to resist or contradict. You will be betrayed even by parents, brothers, relatives and friends, and they will put some of you to death. All men will hate you because of me. But not a hair of your head will perish. By standing firm you will gain life" (Luke 21:15-19).

Explore the Word

Read Luke 21:1-38.

In today's Scripture reading, Jesus prophesies that the Temple and everything around Him will be torn down. Then He points out that the Temple is a place to worship God. But if the people refuse God, what good is it? It becomes nothing but a worthless shell, another empty ritual for "churchianity."

The men ask for signs as to when this destruction will take place. Instead of a definite date, Jesus gives them events that will lead up to it. Though He's referring to the destruction of Jerusalem in A.D. 70, keep in mind that, according to the Book of Revelation, many of the same events will also happen before His second coming.[9]

Jesus warns that many will say they are Christians or even that they are the Messiah. He goes on to say that there will be many wars, famines, plagues, even signs from heaven; but that we are not to worry. God is in control, and He will protect the faithful.

It's definitely hard to accept and most certainly unpleasant to think about. But, like it or not, even committed Christians will suffer from time to time. In fact, recent studies indicate that more than 60 percent of the world is either under some sort of religious persecution or is about to fall under that persecution.

Why? "When the light comes the darkness must depart," explains Charles H. Spurgeon. "Where truth is, the lie must flee. If the lie remains, there will be a severe conflict, because truth cannot and will not lower its standard. If you follow Christ, all the hounds of the world will yelp at your heels."[10]

When the pressure heats up, what should we do?

Live the Word

- **Trust Jesus.** Scripture assures us that we shouldn't be afraid—just faithful. We will even have many opportunities to share Jesus with an unsaved world, and Christ will give us the words.
- **Evaluate your weak points, then take action.** "Let us throw off everything that hinders . . . and let us run with perseverance the race marked out for us" (Hebrews 12:1).

MY PRAYER:

MY THOUGHTS:

Community

Finding Your Identity in Christ

"At my school, if you're not in the right clique, forget it. Yet I'm a Christian—so I'm not supposed to get pulled into this way of thinking. But it's hard. Any clues on what I should do?"

Examine the Word

For we are God's workmanship, created in Christ Jesus to do good works, which God prepared in advance for us to do (Ephesians 2:10).

Explore the Word

Read Psalm 139:13-16.

Cliques. They're everywhere. Groups of guys and girls who never seem to cross an invisible line that separates the classes.

Set foot on a public school campus, and you see them. The cool kids (usually the jocks and prom queens, right?) claim one part of the school; the skaters, surfers, and metal heads hang out in another; while the science and computer kids try to lay low somewhere in the shadows.

How about YOU? Where do you fit into the picture? Do you feel as if every eye is on YOU—like you're the featured act in today's teenage freak show? Guess what? You're NOT a freak—or a zero. And despite what herd you run with, your life counts.

The real freaks are the ones who stay focused on the moment, the guys and girls who don't care about anything except "looking out for number one." In reality, your life is priceless. You are like a valuable masterpiece—an incredible, unique work of art created by God for a purpose much greater than parties and popularity.

LIVE THE WORD

- **Don't lose your identity.** It's OK to express yourself through the clothes you wear or to excel at a sport or a hobby. But if you try to base your total identity on those things, you'll end up losing your identity. What's more, you'll end up bitterly disappointed.
- **Let God be God.** Ask Him to tear down idols in your life—a relationship, a job, a possession . . . anything that you value more than Him. Keep in mind that, in the world's eyes, your identity is wrapped up in what you do, how smart or athletic you are, and how you look. But in God's eyes, what matters is who you are—His child.
- **Find yourself in Christ.** Our Lord wants the very best for you. His plans for you are even better than your wildest dreams. Jesus doesn't look at you and say, "This is who you are—and who you'll always be." Instead, He says, "Just imagine who you can become!"

MY PRAYER:

MY THOUGHTS:

Authentic Faith

"I don't want to be a phony Christian—someone who acts no different than unbelievers. How can I be different? What's the key to truly walking my talk?"

Examine the Word

Dear friends, I urge you, as aliens and strangers in the world, to abstain from sinful desires, which war against your soul. Live such good lives among the pagans that, though they accuse you of doing wrong, they may see your good deeds and glorify God on the day he visits us (1 Peter 2:11-12).

Explore the Word

Read 1 Peter 2:1-12.

Live as an alien—someone who is set apart from the world. A Christian's walk, talk, and mind-set simply cannot mirror the world. We're called to be different. Of course, this is much easier said than done, right? After all, who in their right mind would dare to stand out from the crowd? Conformity is much safer.

Yet as a follower of Christ, you've been called to be different. Your values are not the same as the world in which you live. You're becoming more like the Savior and less a part of planet Earth.

Here's how the Bible instructs you to live: "Be imitators of God, therefore, as dearly loved children and live a life of love, just as Christ loved us and gave himself up for us as a fragrant offering and sacrifice to God" (Ephesians 5:1-2).

Live the Word

- **Keep looking up.** It's easy to be more concerned with what others think of us than what God thinks of us. When this happens, we need to remind ourselves that the opinions of our friends on what is good and right will change many times in the next few years. However, what God thinks is good and right will never change! That's what we should desire to be like.

- **Weigh the balance on your friends.** We all want to fit in with the crowd. Sometimes that means we are asked to compromise our values. Carefully consider what your friends are asking you to do. If you are continually asked to compromise what you believe in to be with them, then maybe it's time to find some new friends who will support and encourage you.
- **Ask others to hold you accountable.** Sometimes we may not even realize that what we are saying and doing are at odds. Having an accountability partner who is not afraid to tell us the truth when things don't match up can help us live a more consistent life.

MY PRAYER:

MY THOUGHTS:

Day 33

Reflecting Christ's Face

"I truly want to reflect Christ's face to others. What must I do?"

Examine the Word

"Do not judge, and you will not be judged. Do not condemn, and you will not be condemned. Forgive, and you will be forgiven. Give, and it will be given to you" (Luke 6:37-38).

Explore the Word

Read Luke 6:37-49.

In today's Scripture reading, Jesus warns the people to stay away from the Pharisees. They're blind, He says. If we follow blind guides, we will fall into holes in the ground. But if we follow Him, He promises to lead us to eternal life.

Jesus wants us to know the truth. He wants us to understand that real satisfaction can't be found in relationships, money, popularity, or inflated brain cells. Our most urgent need isn't the latest computer game or a date for the prom. It is the life that only God can give.

What's more, we need to draw upon strength from Christ. We need the strength God gives through the Word, prayer, fellowship, and worship.

Finally, Jesus tells us to build our houses with firm foundations in Him, not like those who go for the quick payoff. Sand castles may look great and are a snap to build, but they're short-term investments. One big wave or sudden rainstorm, and it is all over. Jesus encourages us to build on His rock, His firm foundation with materials that will last.

Live the Word

- **Have some backbone.** It's safe to say that if most of us knew there wouldn't be any social (or sometimes, economic) consequences when we attempt to represent the Christian faith, we wouldn't hesitate to stand up for God. But because there *are* consequences, many of us keep silent or act all wishy-washy.

  What's more, too many teens think that simply because they're Christians, they're supposed to be accepting about everything. But that's not necessarily true. Jesus *never* asks us to accept that which goes against His holy Word. In fact, He wants us to speak up. But mostly, He wants us to live our faith.

- **Examine your attitude.** Do others notice the "truth" in you? Do they know you follow Christ? Do they see in you the life, joy, and peace that only God can give?

- **Examine your life.** Do you have the courage to stick up for Jesus Christ in the face of opposition—or do you find your faith being trampled by your friends? Why, or why not?

- **Build on the Rock.** If you're depending on anything or anyone other than Jesus Christ to give you real life and ultimate fulfillment, know that your life is stuck in sinking sand. Jesus Christ is the only solid foundation. Make a change. Seek Him. Trust Him. When people look at your life, make sure they see someone with a sincere heart—not a guy or girl hiding behind a mask.

My Prayer:

My Thoughts:

Focus on the Truth

"How should I lead my friends to absolute truth? So many are caught up in worldly philosophies."

Examine the Word

Immediately, something like scales fell from Saul's eyes, and he could see again (Acts 9:18).

Explore the Word

Read Acts 9:1-19.

Saul of Tarsus had an incredible truth encounter on the road to Damascus. He stood face-to-face with the risen Christ, and his life was forever changed.

> As he neared Damascus on his journey, suddenly a light from heaven flashed around him. He fell to the ground and heard a voice say to him, "Saul, Saul, why do you persecute me?"
>
> "Who are you, Lord?" Saul asked.
>
> "I am Jesus, whom you are persecuting," he replied. "Now get up and go into the city, and you will be told what you must do."
>
> The men traveling with Saul stood there speechless; they heard the sound but did not see anyone. Saul got up from the ground, but when he opened his eyes he could see nothing. So they led him by the hand into Damascus *(Acts 9:3-8)*.

When Saul regained his sight, he was a new man. A short time later (Acts 13:9 to be exact), he got a new name: Paul. The Lord gave him an important assignment: tell others about the awesome good news of Jesus Christ. Paul learned to make his work a priority and placed it above everything—ridicule, abuse, peer pressure, embarrassment . . . even the possibility of losing friends.

LIVE THE WORD

- ❖ **Get your eyes off the world.** Being a Christian is the most exciting, most energizing, most fulfilling adventure anybody could ever hope to embark on. Following Jesus isn't a chore or a hassle. It's a privilege! Commit right now to trusting Jesus with your whole heart. Ask Him to help you steer clear of the world's lies and to be firmly grounded in His truth.
- ❖ **Set your sights on the truth.** Understand that following Christ is not a passing fad. It's a step-by-step, day-by-day *commitment.* And as C. S. Lewis explains, God is the Mind and the Power behind the Moral Law of the Universe. "It is after you have realized that there is a real Moral Law, and a Power behind the law, and that you have broken that law and put yourself wrong with that Power—it is after all this, and not a moment sooner, that Christianity begins to talk."[11]
- ❖ **Be bold about what you believe.** God doesn't want you to hide your faith from the world. You're called to "go into all the world" with the Good News. That could mean going next door and sharing Jesus with your neighbor, your friends at school, or even your own family. Commit right now to letting God's love shine through your life so others will come to Him. Christians aren't the ones missing out on good times . . . *the world is.*

MY PRAYER:

MY THOUGHTS:

No More "Churchianity"

"When Sunday morning rolls around, I never feel like going to church. Why is it so important to worship God with the rest of the church? Why can't I do it on my own?"

Examine the Word

Consequently, you are no longer foreigners and aliens, but fellow citizens with God's people and members of God's household, built on the foundation of Jesus himself as the chief cornerstone. In him the whole building is joined together and rises to become a holy temple being built together to become a dwelling in which God lives by his Spirit (Ephesians 2:19-22).

Explore the Word

Read Ephesians 2:11-22.

As the apostle Paul explains in today's scripture passage, *you are the church*, "built on the foundation of Jesus himself as the chief cornerstone." And as a Christian, *you* are a holy temple—a dwelling in which God lives by His Spirit.

By itself, a church facility is just a bunch of bricks and windows and doors. But add to it the *real* holy temple—YOU—and the building becomes a *church*, a sanctuary inhabited by God himself; a sacred house of worship where the Creator and the created commune.

How would you describe your church—a crowded building . . . or a holy family of believers? Since you are the church, why bother setting foot in a church building? After all, can't we worship God just as effectively on our own?

Let's be honest. We all wake up from time to time on Sunday with the strong temptation to worship at "First Church of the Water Bed." But if we're wise, we fight off the temptation.

Here are two key reasons why church attendance is important:

There's no such thing as the lone ranger Christian. Worshiping God is meant to be shared with others. Even if you can't understand everything the pastor says—or if you can't find the Book of Malachi if your life depended upon it—spending time in church teaches you that God's family is a whole lot bigger than your own. And get this: heaven is going be packed with all kinds of people praising and worshiping God. Church is a good place to prepare. What's more, our church family keeps us accountable.

Going to church allows you to serve others. Get involved and serve at your church. God wants you to see it as an honor, not a drag. Why? Because He's calling you to deal with His people, the flock whom He loves. It's your chance to serve Him by serving others. Think of church as your training ground. As you walk through the doors, expect to learn something new, to encourage others, and to be encouraged. Most of all, expect to commune with your Creator.

Live the Word

- **Don't settle for meaningless ritual.** Christ came to end "religion." He came to destroy meaningless ritual and replace it with a dynamic, on-fire *relationship*—a relationship with God himself.
- **Don't view church attendance as a cure for insomnia.** The choice is yours: you can keep Christianity as nothing more than a religion—keep it boring and dull by playing it safe, by going through the ceremonial motions and traditions of "churchianity"—or you can begin pursuing Jesus and His transforming *power.*
- **Fight the temptation to sleep in on Sunday mornings.** Make church attendance a priority. God wants to shape the mature Christian inside of you.

My Prayer:

My Thoughts:

Handling Hard Times

"Lately, my life has been one struggle after another. I know that being a Christian doesn't mean everything is going to be smooth all the time, but I feel so overwhelmed. How can I cope?"

Examine the Word

We are hard pressed on every side, but not crushed; perplexed, but not in despair; persecuted, but not abandoned; struck down, but not destroyed (2 Corinthians 4:8-9).

Explore the Word

Read 2 Corinthians 4:7-18.

Some mornings we wake up and can't help but feel as though our life is in the path of a speeding freight train. Our circumstances may seem hopeless, and we feel frightened and alone. Doubts scream in our minds. *Get up—and run! Or be flattened beyond recognition!*

But the Bible tells us something different: "Stay put! Pray. And trust God." Good advice. In fact, here's what Paul tells us in 2 Corinthians 4:17-18, "For our light and momentary troubles are achieving for us an eternal glory that far outweighs them all. So we fix our eyes not on what is seen, but on what is unseen. For what is seen is temporary, but what is unseen is eternal."

Regardless of your circumstances, God can set you free if you allow Him. He won't always take away the problems or temptations, but He *will* faithfully enter the difficulty with you and provide a way out.

Live the Word

❖ **Jesus shares your pain.** He puts himself in your shoes and feels everything that you feel. He is the Father of "suffering with," and the God of all comfort! When He comes beside you and offers the strength to take your next step, you learn to walk with fellow sufferers—to let their pain become your pain.

❖ **Keep in mind that God fully understands that His people battle through periods of doubt and fear—especially during tough trials.** His Son went through difficult times. Think about Gethsemane. Jesus prayed, anguished, and sweated blood. However, He followed the Father's plan. He came as a man and lived on earth—to save us. He has compassion for His people. It's not what you did or didn't do that counts, it's what He did for you. All He asks is that you let Him into your heart. He stands, knocks, and patiently waits with open arms and listening ears. Won't you let Him in?

MY PRAYER:

MY THOUGHTS:

Servanthood—Part 1

"How can a believer call himself *Christian* if he or she is not committed to serving others? This is how people see Christ in us."

Examine the Word

So we rebuilt the wall till all of it reached half its height, for the people worked with all their heart (Nehemiah 4:6).

Explore the Word

Read Nehemiah 4:1-23.

It's an incredible sight!

Stretched out before Nehemiah, all along Jerusalem's broken walls, are hundreds of men clutching weapons with one hand and making repairs with the other. Half of the busy crew are working tirelessly day and night, rebuilding the crumbled structures, while other men—equipped with spears, bows, shields, and armor—watch and wait for the enemy.

Nehemiah and his workers have confronted what looks like an impossible challenge: rebuilding Jerusalem's toppled walls in the face of fierce opposition.

Striking a balance between prayer and action, this hero of the faith doesn't give up. He has armed the workers with weapons, positioned armies all around Jerusalem, and has commanded his Jewish brothers and sisters to persevere with the hope of God in their hearts.

In the process, Nehemiah has lifted the spirits of a despondent people and has restored their faith—just as he is restoring their city. His actions speak loudly to all generations: The best way to resist the Lord's enemies is to get on with the Lord's work.

LIVE THE WORD

- **Take the time to look around you.** Someone needs you. Someone at church, at school, at home. There's that 74-year-old man whose wife has Alzheimer's disease . . . he needs someone to talk to. Then there's that couple with a handicapped child . . . they really could use a break. You don't have to head off on a mission trip to Panama to serve God. Do it every day in lots of little ways—such as taking the time to talk to that elderly man or volunteering to baby-sit for that couple with a handicapped child.
- **Get involved!** At church, at school, in your community . . . and be salt and light to the world.

MY PRAYER:

MY THOUGHTS:

Servanthood—Part 2

"Faith heroes like Nehemiah are examples of believers who are socially minded. What can I do to make a difference in this world?"

Examine the Word

"The King will reply, 'I tell you the truth, whatever you did for one of the least of these brothers of mine, you did for me'" (Matthew 25:40).

Explore the Word

Read Matthew 25:31-46.

New York City is much different from the Jerusalem of Nehemiah's time. (Remember we talked about Nehemiah on day 37.) Yet the "walls of morality" in much of this modern metropolis are cracked and worn—bombarded by pain, despair, and sin.

In one Manhattan neighborhood called Hell's Kitchen, anything goes. And from 42nd Street to Times Square, pimps—often decked out in gold chains, wide-brimmed hats, and $500 Bally shoes—preen along the streets, while their "ladies" seduce the young and the vulnerable. Eleven-year-olds weave in and out of the crowds, peddling everything from weed to heroin. "Take your pick—'ludes, crack, dust. I've got your high."

Stubble-faced winos rest their heads in the gutters, while bag ladies, dressed in filthy, ill-fitting clothes, shuffle by with their earthly possessions stored away in shopping carts or tied in bundles to their backs.

The young and the old, the homeless, the runaways, the lost, and the forgotten all lead a bleak existence in the clutches of a brutal enemy—the street. But teenagers are fighting back. A number of young Christians from the urban enclaves of New York have taken Nehemiah's message to heart and are bringing light and hope to some schools and neighborhoods.

For nearly 33 years, young men and women associated with Urban Youth Alliance, a Harlem-based Christian ministry operated by high school and college students, have put their faith into action, taking the gospel to more than 30 public schools throughout the Big Apple.

Modeling Nehemiah's example, the group's leaders see to it that work and prayer go hand in hand. They "put on the full armor of God" (Ephesians 6:11) and step out in faith, sometimes confronting tough opposition.

Many of the students face daily battles from school administration. Even though the teens have a legal right to meet on school grounds and hold Bible studies, some faculty members don't welcome them. A lot of parents don't want a Christian witness on campus, either.

At one high school, the administration wouldn't allow the students to bring Bibles on campus or to pray. The youths didn't give up. Instead, they forged ahead and found some creative ways to get around their temporary barriers.

"We would work out the Bible studies in advance and typed the scriptures on paper," says Nancy, one club member. "We'd also sing our prayers. Eventually, we won the respect of school officials—and have managed to bring God's light in a spiritually dark place."

With a heavy dose of prayer and Christian service, these inner-city teens are holding their ground for Christ. Nehemiah would be pleased.

Live the Word

- **Be Christ's hands and feet.** From His birth to His death on a cross, Jesus' life is a shining example of humility and service. He reached out to those who no one else wanted around. He brought love to the unloved, hope to the hopeless. How about you? Ask God to help you find at least one non-Christian person you can reach through prayer and service.
- **Accept the call to care.** Think about modern-day outcasts: the glassy-eyed burnout at school or the geek who's always picked on in the halls. Would Jesus visit these people? Would He know their names, care about them, tell them stories? He would—and you should too. How? Find an outcast around you, and look for ways that you can affect his or her life.

My Prayer:

My Thoughts:

God-Sized Love

"Have Christians—especially Christian males—forgotten how to love? It's sad when unbelievers view the church as angry, judgmental, and cliquish."

Examine the Word

"A new command I give you: Love one another. As I have loved you, so you must love one another. By this all men will know that you are my disciples, if you love one another" (John 13:34-35).

Explore the Word

Read 1 Corinthians 13:1-13.

Examine how love is supposed to be expressed. "Love is patient, love is kind. It does not envy, it does not boast, it is not proud. It is not rude, it is not self-seeking, it is not easily angered, it keeps no record of wrongs. Love does not delight in evil but rejoices with the truth. It always protects, always trusts, always hopes, always perseveres. Love never fails" (1 Corinthians 13:4-8).

Is this the kind of love Christians are called to share? Actually, it is. God loves us despite our flaws and shortcomings. He is secure in who He is. Therefore, He loves us unconditionally and without giving a second thought to our failures.

In his book *A Gift of Love*, Dr. Charles Stanley writes: "He knows that there will be times when we look and act very unholy. Our misguided actions do not erase or stop the love of God. Sin can separate us from His blessings and intimate fellowship, but there is never a time when God withholds His love."[12]

Live the Word

- **Understand that our love for others is evidence of our love for God.** And when we love others unconditionally—forgiving them and reaching out to them—we can approach Jesus confidently in prayer. It is our assurance that our prayers will be heard. (Check out 1 John 4:15.)

❖ **Communicate ultimate love: Say to your non-Christian friends:** "For God is love and He sent His Son to save us from our sin. Christ was the Lamb of God slain for us, who rose from the dead and now lives on the throne. Through His grace we know He will touch and heal our pain and give us strength to meet each day. With the shield of faith and the sword of the Word we will win the fight. Our foe will not beat us when we stand firm and true."

❖ **Demonstrate ultimate love:** Share the love you experience through Christ with your friends—just as Jesus "[laid] down his life for his friends" (John 15:13). Let your speech and actions be a clear message of God's salvation and grace and love. This is the essence of true Christian love.

MY PRAYER:

MY THOUGHTS:

Pass On the Good News

"When it comes to witnessing, I feel clueless, speechless, and totally ineffective. What's the right way to share my faith?"

Examine the Word

In the presence of God and of Christ Jesus, who will judge the living and the dead, and in view of his appearing and his kingdom, I give you this charge: Preach the Word; be prepared in season and out of season; correct, rebuke and encourage—with great patience and careful instruction (2 Timothy 4:1-2).

Explore the Word

Read 2 Corinthians 2:12–3:6.

Jesus didn't call us to hide in a Christian huddle or to be part of His "secret service." As Christians, we've grounded our lives on what the Bible says, which means we're convinced that humankind is more than just a cosmic accident. Jesus Christ is transforming our lives, and we've got to tell the world about it.

Sharing our faith should be the most natural thing in the world, because it's really nothing more than telling someone else the story of what God has done for us. When we talk about Jesus with another person, we are sharing our faith. When we tell the story of our spiritual journey in front of a group, we are sharing our faith. When we tell people about Jesus in a letter or E-mail, we are sharing our faith. In fact, the Lord actually wants us to create occasions in which to talk about Him, seizing every opportunity to communicate our faith, witnessing where we are.[13]

Live the Word

- **Be real with God—and others.** Too many teens mistakenly believe that God doesn't want them to be honest about their lives. They think that He will be upset if they tell Him how they really feel. However, the

Scriptures tell us that God does not want us to be superficial in our relationship with Him, with others, or in our own life. In Psalm 51:6, David writes, "Surely you desire truth in the inner parts; you teach me wisdom in the inmost place."

❖ **Be honest about your pain, confusion, or doubt**—even with people you're trying to reach with the gospel. You aren't expected to have all the answers—just a committed, searching heart.

The fact is, God desires truth and honesty at the deepest level and wants you to experience His love, forgiveness, and power in *all* areas of your life. Experiencing His love doesn't mean that all of your thoughts, emotions, and behaviors will be pleasant and pure. It means that you can be *real*, feeling pain and joy, love and anger, confidence and confusion. It's this kind of honesty that will attract others to the gospel.

MY PRAYER:

MY THOUGHTS:

COMPASSION

Day 41

Let Your Lifestyle Be a Witness

"Actions speak louder than words—especially for my generation. Any suggestions on how I can let my life be a witness?"

Examine the Word

Be very careful, then, how you live—not as unwise but as wise, making the most of every opportunity, because the days are evil. Therefore do not be foolish, but understand what the Lord's will is. Do not get drunk on wine, which leads to debauchery. Instead, be filled with the Spirit. Speak to one another with psalms, hymns and spiritual songs. Sing and make music in your heart to the Lord, always giving thanks to God the Father for everything, in the name of our Lord Jesus Christ (Ephesians 5:15-20).

Explore the Word

Read 2 Corinthians 2:12-17; 3:1-6.

What does your "letter" say to others? Is your walk in sync with your talk? Is your life a reflection of Jesus?

Witnessing is all about telling and showing others what Jesus is like. You can tell them by what you say, but you show them by your own conduct.

Discover ways of allowing the Holy Spirit to touch others through your lifestyle instead of just blending into the crowd. "Do your best to present yourself to God as one approved, a workman who does not need to be ashamed and who correctly handles the word of truth" (2 Timothy 2:15).

Live the Word

❖ **When people look at your life, make sure they see . . .**

. . . someone constantly dying to Jesus.

. . . a person of integrity who dares to put his or her life on the line for the gospel.

. . . a teen with a sincere heart—not a guy or girl hiding behind a mask.

❖ **Be bold.** Never let fear hold you back from befriending an unbeliever. Consider the observations of legendary evangelist Billy Graham: "It is fear that makes us unwilling to listen to another's point of view, fear that our own ideas may be attacked. Jesus had no such fear, no such pettiness of viewpoint, no need to fence Himself off for His own protection. He knew the difference between graciousness and compromise and we would do well to learn from Him."[14]

MY PRAYER:

MY THOUGHTS:

Day 42

Be an Encourager

"A lot of teens I know—even Christian ones—are so negative. I don't believe this type of attitude represents Christ very well. How can I be different?"

Examine the Word

May the words of my mouth and the meditation of my heart be pleasing in your sight, O LORD, my Rock and my Redeemer (Psalm 19:14).

Explore the Word

Read Psalm 19.

The two main centers of obedience to God are your heart and your mouth. That's why David was concerned that the words of his mouth and the meditation of his heart be pleasing in God's sight (Psalm 19:14). He knew that if he could just let his Heavenly Father take control of his heart and his mouth, he could live a holy life, a life that would be a testimony to God's glory and grace.

Consider the words of your mouth. Does your speech encourage and empower—or does it wound and destroy? Do you communicate hope, or do you occasionally spray others with hateful graffiti such as insults and put-downs?

Live the Word

❖ **Tell them the truth about who they are.** Be one of the few who remind their friends of their strengths and abilities.

❖ **A few friendly put-downs often become a habit.** Cut back on the cuts!

❖ **Be a defender of your friends when they're in front of you or when someone is talking behind their backs.** Point them to the One who will always tell them the truth.

MY PRAYER:

MY THOUGHTS:

Day 43

Be a Real Christian in the Real World

"The world needs to see Christians who treat people with dignity and respect—not believers who treat individuals like 'projects.' We need to see others with Christ's compassionate eyes. Any ideas on how to do this?"

Examine the Word

"If the world hates you, keep in mind that it hated me first" (John 15:18).

Explore the Word

Read John 15:18-27.

It's not easy to stand up for what you believe when you feel outnumbered. Yet keeping your mouth shut or alienating yourself from the world aren't the answers either.

While there isn't a simple formula for sharing your beliefs, it all boils down to this: if you identify yourself with Christ, and if you're confident abou[t] what you believe and where you're headed as a Christian, it will be much more natural to live your faith around non-Christian friends. In other words, confidence is the key. If you're not uptight about being a Christian, your friends won't be bothered about it either.

Check Your Pulse . . .

. . . When the pressure hits, do you catch yourself hiding your faith or speaking up (even at the risk of being unpopular)?

. . . How can you develop more courage?

. . . Do you have an eternal perspective? (In other words, do you care more about pleasing God or pleasing the world?)

Live the Word

- **Never develop a holier-than-thou attitude.** Alienating the world by preaching a bunch of "dos" and "don'ts," or by speaking in Christianese—a languag[e] most nonbelieving earthlings don't understand—isn't what Christ has in min[d] for your life.

❖ **Step out with confidence.** The world desperately needs to see a solid Christian example. But if Christianity is lived only within the safety of the church walls and tight circles of like-minded friends, how can we make an impact? How can God use us in the lives of those who are blind to the truth?

❖ **Never keep quiet and blend in.** Too many Christian teens choose this approach. They want to be members of God's secret service, so their speech and actions are no different from those of non-Christians. And when God becomes the topic of conversation, they clam up.

❖ **Speak up with confidence.** People respect someone who is committed to what they believe, someone who isn't wishy-washy. Unlike keeping quiet or alienating yourself, this approach offers Christians the most honest and challenging lifestyle.

MY PRAYER:

MY THOUGHTS:

Day 44

Lead Them to the Savior

"What's the greatest thing I can do for a non-Christian?"

Examine the Word

Therefore, since we are surrounded by such a great cloud of witnesses, let us throw off everything that hinders and the sin that so easily entangles, and let us run with perseverance the race marked out for us. Let us fix our eyes on Jesus, the author and perfecter of our faith, who for the joy set before him endured the cross, scorning its shame, and sat down at the right hand of the throne of God. Consider him who endured such opposition from sinful men, so that you will not grow weary and lose heart (Hebrews 12:1-3).

Explore the Word

Read John 6:22-29.

When the crowds catch up to Jesus, He points out that they really didn't search for Him because of the miracles—they came because they ate the bread He'd provided and were filled.

But He explains that, even though they were satisfied by the bread, they shouldn't be so concerned about physical food. It spoils. He has a different type of food, a food for the soul that satisfies a deeper hunger—a food that satisfies the hunger for love, for truth, for fulfillment. Most importantly, He points out that it is a food only He can provide.

The people immediately want to know what they can do to earn this love, this fulfilled life. In short, they want to know what they can do to earn God's favor. Jesus' answer couldn't be simpler: "Believe in Me."

Live the Word

❖ **Evaluate your motives.** Are you a Christian because it's sort of the family thing to do? Do you attend youth group because that's where all your friends hang out? Or do you truly trust Christ as your Lord and Savior?

❖ **Spend some time in prayer, asking Jesus to help you hunger for Him, not the world.** Ask Him to quench your thirst (you know, with stuff like peace, joy, fulfillment, happiness, spiritual wisdom, strength).

MY PRAYER:

MY THOUGHTS:

Day 45

Christlike Compassion

"It's a touching scene in the Bible when Jesus washes His disciples' feet. How should I live out this example in my life?"

Examine the Word

When he had finished washing their feet, he put on his clothes and returned to his place. "Do you understand what I have done for you?" he asked them. "You call me 'Teacher' and 'Lord,' and rightly so, for that is what I am. Now that I, your Lord and Teacher, have washed your feet, you also should wash one another's feet. I have set you an example that you should do as I have done for you" (John 13:12-15).

Explore the Word

Read John 13:1-17.

Jesus has fewer than 24 hours left on earth. Take a good look at the image He gives His disciples: the Savior with a towel in His hands. The Creator kneeling before His creation, lathering up their feet, rinsing them off, drying them! Incredible! It's a perfect picture of servanthood.

Christ demonstrates His love. The custom at this time called for the host's servant to wash the guests' feet. But since there was no host where Jesus and His friends were eating, there was no servant. Other Gospel accounts talk about how the disciples had been arguing over which of them was the greatest—so there's a good chance most of them were pretty worried about who was going to get the bottom-of-the-barrel job of feet washing.

Christ demonstrates that the only way to be saved is through Him. We need to be washed by the Lord. Then we need to take up the towel, go into the world, and do likewise—communicating the good news of Jesus Christ.

LIVE THE WORD

❖ **Ask Jesus to help you . . .**

. . . give up your own will for the will of God.

. . . live daily a life of spiritual sacrifice for the glory of Christ.

. . . strive to be consistently obedient to our Lord.

❖ **Follow Christ's example of true greatness.** It's not the world leaders, the Wall Street wizards, the Hollywood superstars, or the Super Bowl survivors. It's not even the great spiritual leaders of our times. These aren't who God considers to be great. Instead, according to the Lord, it's often just the opposite. According to Jesus, "Whoever wants to become great among you must be your servant, and whoever wants to be first must be your slave—just as the Son of Man did not come to be served, but to serve, and to give his life as a ransom for many" (Matthew 20:26-28).

MY PRAYER:

MY THOUGHTS:

NOTES

1. Bill Myers, Michael Ross, *Faith Encounter* (Eugene, Oreg.: Harvest House Publishers, 1999), 112.

2. Max Lucado, *He Still Moves Stones* (Nashville: Word, 1993), 110.

3. C. S. Lewis, *Mere Christianity* (New York: HarperCollins, 2001), 121-22.

4. Henry Blackaby, *Experiencing God* (Nashville: Broadman and Holman, 1998), 310.

5. Michael Ross, *Faith That Breathes* (Uhrichsville, Ohio: Barbour Publishing, 2003), 54.

6. Max Lucado, *The Great House of God* (Nashville: Word, 1997), x.

7. Myers and Ross, *Faith Encounter*, 197-98.

8. Charles Stanley, *A Gift of Love* (Nashville: Thomas Nelson Publishers, 2001), 5.

9. Myers and Ross, *Faith Encounter*, 171.

10. Charles H. Spurgeon, *Morning and Evening* (Nashville: Thomas Nelson Publishers, 1994), December 28, evening.

11. Lewis, *Mere Christianity*, 31.

12. Charles Stanley, *A Gift of Love* (Thomas Nelson, Nashville, 2001), 191.

13. Terry Brown and Michael Ross, *Communicate* (Uhrichsville, Ohio: Barbour Publishing, 2002), 19.

14. Billy Graham, *Unto the Hills* (Dallas: Word Publishing, 1986), 123-24.